The Unequal Hours

The Unequal Hours

Moments of Being in the Natural World

LINDA UNDERHILL

The University of Georgia Press *Athens and London*

© 1999 by the University of Georgia Press
Athens, Georgia 30602
All rights reserved
Designed by Sandra Strother Hudson
Set in 10.5 on 15 Aldus with Delphin display
by G & S Typesetters, Inc.
Printed and bound by Maple-Vail
The paper in this book meets the guidelines for
permanence and durability of the Committee on
Production Guidelines for Book Longevity of the
Council on Library Resources.

Printed in the United States of America
03 02 01 00 99 C 5 4 3 2 1

Library of Congress Cataloging in Publication Data
Underhill, Linda.
The unequal hours : moments of being in the natural world /
Linda Underhill.
p.   cm.
ISBN 0-8203-2040-4 (alk. paper)
1. Allegany County (N.Y.)—Description and travel.
2. Underhill, Linda.   3. Allegany County (N.Y.)—
Biography.   4. Allegany County (N.Y.)—Social life
and customs.   5. Natural history—New York (State)—
Allegany County.   I. Title.
F127.A4U54   1999
508.747'84—dc21   98-22322
                                                  CIP

British Library Cataloging in Publication Data available
On the title page: *Five,* graphite drawing © 1981 by
Nancy Batson Carter.

For my parents

ED and HELEN

who were my first teachers

Everything in nature

invites us constantly

to be what we are.

GRETEL EHRLICH, *The Solace of Open Spaces*

Contents

Acknowledgments

For guiding me in my wanderings, I am grateful to Allegany County Historian Craig Braack and Houghton College professor Jim Wolfe. I owe thanks to Greg Livadas and Andy Glanzman for giving me High Hopes. I am indebted to David McKain for his thoughtful comments on the manuscript in its early stages, and to the staff of the David Howe Library in Wellsville and the Herrick Memorial Library at Alfred University for their help with my research. I also wish to express my appreciation to Trudie Calvert for her thoughtful and meticulous editing.

Portions of the manuscript appeared originally, in slightly different form, in *Artifacts*, the *Olean Times Herald*, the *Sylvan Review*, and *Under the Sun*. I thank the editors of these publications for encouraging my work along the way.

Finally, for his invaluable suggestions on developing my ideas, and for his constant love and support, I owe everything to my husband, Bill Underhill.

The Unequal Hours

The Moment

Moment after moment, we find our own way.
SHUNRYU SUZUKI,
Zen Mind, Beginner's Mind

In each day there are tens of thousands of moments, 86,400 of them, to be precise. Most of these thousands of moments pass by with so little notice that we are hardly aware of them. We are too busy making plans for the future, lamenting the time we have wasted in the past, or saying we have no time. We may be alive, and we may be awake, but we live in a state of nonbeing. We are not paying attention to the present.

But there is a moment outside of time, the one Virginia Woolf called the "moment of being." Now and then, she says, from the confusion of everyday life, a clarity emerges, and we see the connections between one thing and another, between one person and another, between one place and another. In such moments, we become aware of how rich is the tapestry of life we wander through. We understand that the world is our home. It is the job of the writer, Woolf says, to receive and to record these moments of being, to find the pattern of meaning in daily life.

Like the sudden moments of illumination in haiku, these are rooted in the ordinary, but they reveal the extraordinary.

In these moments, we are able to capture the sacred, as Willa Cather said in *The Song of the Lark*, "to imprison for a moment the shining, elusive element which is life itself—life hurrying past us and running away, too strong to stop, too sweet to lose."

Beginning in 1991, I began to seek out moments of being where I live and work, in rural western New York. I had already watched for two years as a group of volunteers called the Concerned Citizens of Allegany County successfully fought the efforts of the governor of New York State, Mario Cuomo, and his siting commission to place a low-level nuclear waste dump here. Allegany County was chosen, no doubt, because few people in our own state have heard of it. It is nevertheless home to three small colleges, one of which—Alfred University—is where my husband, Bill, and I both teach. Far from New York City and Albany and Buffalo, Allegany County borders Cattaraugus County to the west and Pennsylvania to the south. It has no cities but many small towns, no amusement parks or shopping malls but many acres of forest, no race tracks or casinos or ski resorts but many streams, creeks, and ponds. Its natural environment, the Concerned Citizens argued, was its greatest resource, and they wanted it protected from the possible contamination of a nuclear waste dump. All over the county, signs and bumper stickers sprouted urging us to "Bump the Dump." Through meetings, teach-ins and editorials, newsletters, concerts, and marches, the waste dump proposal was debated. Early in 1991, there was a stand-off between protesters blocking the commission's access to the proposed site for the dump and the state police ordered to clear them from the area. The governor blinked. He called the siting commission home, and they have not been back to Allegany County since.

I was newly married, and I had never before been so far removed from urban life. I grew up in Pittsburgh and had spent most of my life in cities. I was only vaguely aware of the growing environmental movement. And what I did hear almost always applied to remote wilderness areas, for the most part places where I never expected to live or even to visit. I had never thought about a battle for "the environment" occurring in my own backyard.

I decided to find out what my new neighbors had fought so hard to save.

So for the next four years, I looked out the windows of my house, wandered the streets of my town, and traveled the roads of the county where the Concerned Citizens had fought their battles. I explored the elements of the natural world that could be found in these ordinary surroundings. I gave myself up to the places Bill and I call home, our house on its three quarters of an acre in the town of Wellsville, and the old farm a few miles away where the family keeps a cabin. I found many moments of being in the natural world—often when I was least expecting them—when I was sweeping our porch, weeding our garden, or simply sitting and looking out at our yard. I felt the touch of water, the movement of wind, and the promptings of memory. I searched for color in a winter landscape and taught myself to see the wild creatures living in my own backyard. I learned about the growth of trees and the symmetry of ice. I studied the meaning of sanctuaries, nature preserves owned and supervised by conservation organizations, as well as ordinary backyard gardens and the acres of land purchased by those with no other purpose than to protect the forest from development.

I found that a wilderness voyage isn't necessary to experience the natural world. "In wilderness is the preservation of the world," said Henry David Thoreau. Yet most of us, after all, do not live in the wilderness. We live in cities and towns, suburbs and subdivisions. Here too, I have learned, is the natural world, and here too is a calling, to find in the most ordinary of places a world worth keeping.

Each of these moments of being, like stones thrown into a pond, sent out ripples of thought and memory to other places, to places I had seen and to places I had only read about and to the stories of ancient people who gave witness to the sacred powers of the natural world. I collected these ripples, too, in the narratives that follow.

These essays describing moments of being in the natural world also pose some questions. How do ordinary people benefit from a relationship with the natural world? And what choices can we make that will improve our environment right here, where we live and work?

On his Independence Day, Thoreau decided to leave home and go to the woods, to live, as he said, "deliberately," to "front only the essential facts of life." His friend Ralph Waldo Emerson said, "Let us not rove, let us sit at home with the cause."

On my Independence Day, I decided to stay at home.

Independence Day

Between one breath time and the next,
between one lifetime and the next,
something waits for a moment.
P. L. TRAVERS, *What the Bee Knows*

This morning I put the final coat of white enamel paint on an old chair I am restoring. The chair is a high stool we found in the kitchen of an abandoned farmhouse on country property belonging to my husband, Bill. It is made of heavy, solid maple, with tooled legs and a short ladder back. When we found it, it was scratched and dull, its paint turned colorless with age. Stripped of the old paint and made shining white again, it is transformed. It makes a fine stool for the kitchen counter in our house in town, a place for a friend to sit and talk to me while I cook, a place for me to linger with morning coffee, a perch for sleepless nights and midnight snacks.

The solid old life of the object must still be underneath, layer upon layer of associations I can only guess at. If only I had a magnifying glass of memory I could hold up to the old wood, what could it tell me of the people who owned this chair, the meals they prepared in their kitchen, the birthday parties, the arguments, the tears, the late nights waiting for a child to come home? How many times did this chair see winter come to the farm and firewood hauled in to warm the old house? Was it made by hand in a workshop on the farm or purchased from the hardware store in town? Once, long before, it was a tree growing in a glade, just like the maples that grow on the hillside behind the old farmhouse now.

Emerging fresh and white again, the old chair reflects the new life of the present moment on a warm morning in July, Independence Day.

Waiting for the paint to dry, I walk outside carrying a pair of scissors to clip a bouquet. The two ravens who live here year-round are flying back and forth squawking loudly, and as I look up at them to see what is the matter I notice that another pair is also flying about, and the residents must be trying to chase the intruders off. This is their home, too. Orange and black viceroy butterflies soar over the roof on a warm breeze, catching the updraft, heading for one of the mini-meadows we have allowed to grow up around the house. Another kind of butterfly I have not yet been able to name is velvety blue, white, and black. It floats right past me at eye level. Innumerable tiny white moths, wasps, beetles, and bees careen through the yard, feeding on the nectar of flowers blooming now. One of the wasps found its way inside this morning as I was working at my desk, and I had to catch it in my pencil cup and carry it outside trapped with a postcard over the cup as it buzzed in annoyance at its captivity, however temporary.

I stoop to clip a few stems of the purple spirea among the hosta in the door yard, and I notice another butterfly perched on a tangle of leaves, legs bent and antennae outstretched as if alive, but unmoving. I poke at it with the tip of my scissors, and then I see that one wing is tattered, and its eyes are dull. How could it give up life, perched on this stem as if only resting, about to take flight again in a moment? We think of death as a struggle, a heroic battle, an ordeal, yet it also comes like this, in the midst of movement, on a warm summer day.

It is a tiger swallowtail, *Papilio glaucus*, the two points of its tails black and shiny, delicate spires at the ends of its veined and scalloped wings. Often, I have found dead butterflies on the street, fallen from treetops, their wings tattered almost beyond recognition. But never before have I seen one so nearly perfect that it might have been alive the moment before. The black and yellow stripes of its wings and its furry body resemble a tiger skin. The outer edges of the hind wings have a blue band scalloped with yellow crescents and two bright orange globes on either end, as if to suggest the phases of the moon.

The black stripes on the wings, a little over an inch long, appear as if made by the brush strokes of a calligrapher's pen dipped in rich black ink on yellow paper, some strokes fat and full, blurred at the edges like a stencil, some mere pencil lines, some fading out to a powdery blur. All of these could be the strokes taught in the study of Chinese ink painting, yet they were made not by an artist trained in a painting class but one that lives in the cells of the butterfly, designing life and painting with DNA.

Before its metamorphosis, while this creature was still a caterpillar, the genes that designed this wing cut away its shape as if from a blank piece of paper and then marked each brush stroke on the butterfly's wing, exactly where it would color the composition. Using a few simple patterns, a few basic shapes, and pigments derived in part from the plants the caterpillar eats, the genes within a butterfly's cells can produce innumerable variations on a theme. Some butterflies have eyespots, and some do not, some have dashes, dots, chevrons, or borders on the wings, and some do not.

What cellular memory guides these choices, changing the caterpillar, slimy and munching on the leaves of our trees, into one of the most beautiful of creation's mysteries, floating free?

This is the secret of the butterfly, the magic of metamorphosis and flight which becomes to us a symbol of the soul, its rebirth and resurrection, its promise of freedom. Thus medieval painters put a butterfly on the Christ child's hand when they depicted him on his mother's lap. Thus the Taoist Chuang Tzu dreamed that he was a butterfly and then wondered if he were dreaming of the butterfly or if the butterfly were dreaming of him.

Some butterflies are plain-Janes, clothed in simple white or pale yellow. Others are gaudy as peacocks, and some even have a wing that resembles a peacock feather, with its iridescent eye. Their wings may be painted brilliant orange and black, sulfurous yellow, copper red, gorgeous green, purple, or blue. They are called painted ladies, mourning cloaks, checkerspots, commas, and question marks. They are called Apollos, Dianas, elfins, nymphs, satyrs, admirals, monarchs, and viceroys. Their colors are made both of pigment and of the structure of the scales overlapping on the butterfly's wing which modify the wavelengths of light striking them to make them look like velvet or satin, glass or metal. Some have colors in the ultraviolet end of the spectrum, seen only by other butterflies or bees. And the butterflies themselves, with the thousand views of their faceted eyes, can see much more than we do. The ultraviolet landing strip on a flower petal beckons to them; the world to them is a symphony of colors we can know only in dreams.

Butterflies use their coloration not merely for art but for protection. They mimic leaf and bark, stem and stone, to give themselves camouflage. They mimic other butterflies known to be poisonous. Their vivid eyespots and stripes may startle an enemy, hypnotizing it long enough for the butterfly to make an escape. The intermittent play of bright patterns on a butterfly's wing as it flits through the air makes it harder to capture than a wing of a single hue would be. The phenomenon is called "dazzling coloration" because it appears to dazzle the butterfly's predators. Butterflies also seem to mimic our own art—or mock it. Some butterfly wings look like shiny metal, some like marble, some like stained glass.

One day not long ago as I crossed the courtyard of our home I noticed what I thought at first was a wedge of wood sitting on the edge of the fence, and while wondering how it got there, I came close enough to see that it was not wood at all but a brown butterfly sitting perfectly still on the ledge. Its veined wings were colored to resemble wood grain, a wedge with edges slightly ragged, like a rough cut, splintered and spiked. This one, however, unlike the tiger swallowtail, was still alive, and when I came too close it took flight, to live at least another day. The average life span of a butterfly is seven to ten days.

I keep the tiger swallowtail on my desk, resting on the leaf just as I found it, wings half folded as if ready for flight, rather than spreading it to lay in a box as Vladimir Nabokov would have done. A lifelong fascination with butterflies led him to chase them over three continents. Nabokov became an expert on the classification *Lycaenidae melissa,* commonly known as the mountain blues, and used them as the inspiration for describing his famous nymph Lolita, with her "downy limbs." "Few things indeed have I known," he says in his autobiography, *Speak, Memory,* "in the way of emotion or appetite, ambition or achievement, that could surpass in richness and strength the excitement of entomological exploration." Standing in a field filled with a rare butterfly he had hunted, he says, was ecstasy, "and behind the ecstasy is something else, which is hard to explain. It is like a momentary vacuum into which rushes all that I love. A sense of oneness with sun and stone."

The first of his captures, when he was seven, was "a splendid, pale-yellow creature with black blotches, blue crenels, and a cinnabar eyespot above each chrome-rimmed black tail." He caught it in a cap and put it in a wardrobe overnight. But it escaped the next morning when the wardrobe was opened by his nurse. Then he learned to use ether to still the butterflies when catching them in his net and to pierce the thorax with a pin and position his captive on a cork-bottomed spreading board covered with thin paper, for display in glass-covered boxes.

I collect my butterflies in memory. I remember the yellow butterfly I saw resting on Bill's shoulder some long minutes one day as he walked ahead of me in the woods, unaware of the stowaway catching a lift. I remember the large brown butterfly with the arc of white moons on its fore wings and the band of iridescent blue on its hind wings that sat for a moment on the chair on my deck, folding and unfolding its wings in the sunlight. And I remember the flock of large orange and black monarchs we watched dance in a field of milkweed behind the old farmhouse one afternoon late in August. They were bound for Mexico, twenty-five hundred miles away. Without habitat like this, the monarchs could not make their annual journey. Generations live and die along the way, feeding on milkweed where they can find it, passing on the memory of the long route in their genes. The development of what were once meadowlands full of wild flowers into shopping centers, parking lots, and lawns threatens their being more than the butterfly hunter's net and bottle of ether.

So we do nothing with our country property, letting the milkweed and the goldenrod, the wild yarrow and the purple thistle grow free. Here there will be no parking lots or vacation homes, no convenience stores or souvenir shops. And in town, we do not chop down the wildflowers some call weeds: Queen Anne's lace, daisies, and dandelions. Here where the house we live in is built there was a meadow years ago, and the land remembers.

In my kitchen, I sit on the old chair with my feet hooked around its tooled legs and look at the tiger swallowtail cupped in my palm. It grows brittle and soon may turn to dust, the final metamorphosis. Then it will become memory. Every one of the ten thousand things will become something else in time. And in every moment, every thing shares life with every other thing. At this moment on Independence Day, the chair, the butterfly, and I, we live here together.

In the Heart of the Wild

Could we not fly too, with broad wings
and with softness, and be all one wing.
VIRGINIA WOOLF, "The Moment: Summer's Night"

I live in a town a dozen miles from any freeways and a good thirty miles from any shopping malls. We have a KMart, a Burger King, and a McDonald's, four banks, three factories, a marching band, and a civic orchestra. There is a fair amount of automobile traffic, enough people and enough business to generate constant comings and goings in noisy vehicles raising dust from the streets of summer and carving ruts in the snows of winter.

Yet I have only to look out the windows of my home, and I am in the heart of the wild. Our house is built on three quarters of an acre, enough space for many trees. Apple, beech, linden, locust, maple, pear, willow, fir, hemlock, spruce, and pine provide shelter and food for things with wings. On a morning in March, I look up from my desk to see a flash of scarlet flight outside my window—something alive, moving through the space of our yard. The night was cool, and the grass bears a paper-thin veneer of frost dissolving rapidly in the bright sun. On the leafless branch of the locust tree at the end of our deck is a bright red cardinal, a welcome sight here since we have more trees than we have the hedges where they like to build their nests. This beautiful creature with its scarlet wings, neat black face mask, and yellow beak perches serenely in the locust tree a moment, enjoying the sunlight and fluffing its feathers. I know his mate, in her dark golden plumage, will be somewhere nearby, although I don't see her. They are rarely apart.

The cardinal has come to this part of the world only recently, a hundred or so years ago. It is one of the few birds whose numbers are growing rather than declining, perhaps for the very reason that it doesn't need trees for its nests. It prefers the edges of woodlands, and these it finds in the hedges and shrubbery that often divide one suburban lot from another.

Our backyard and that of the next house down from ours combine without fences to form a natural habitat of sorts, dotted with trees, bushes, and garden beds, and here we share space with many wild things. Some are the opportunists like blue jays, squirrels, and rabbits, but there are also the cardinal and his mate, a pair of mourning doves, a pair of ravens, and a constantly changing company of other birds. I often see downy woodpeckers searching for insects on the linden tree—their feathers are striped black and white, and the male has a bright red cap on his head. A large patch of thistle attracts goldfinches. Ruby-throated hummingbirds visit the flowers growing in pots on our deck in the summer, and in winter, a host of chickadees, juncos, nuthatches, and grosbeaks come to the feeders I fill with sunflower seeds. There is also a large family of red house finches that has taken up residence in the birdhouse our neighbor built for purple martin.

Many of these creatures stay the winter and keep me company through the dark, cold months. And in a climate where

I would perish if exposed for even one night without shelter, they thrive.

At noon on the coldest day of the year, while the temperature still hovers close to zero, the spruce tree outside my window sparkles in the cold sunlight as if hung with tinsel, its branches drooping with the heavy, wet snow on its branches. The Scotch pine next to it holds only little tufts of snow like cotton balls on its more open branches, reminding me of a Japanese wood-block print I have seen of exactly such a tree, tufted with balls of wet snow, and a colorful pheasant perched jauntily in the foreground, showing off its bright feathers.

I watch a gray mourning dove sitting on the bare branch of an apple tree out in the yard while a frigid wind sweeps the trees, blowing snow into crystalline clouds. The dove stays on its branch, swaying in the wind. Beside the spruce tree the linden spreads graceful, bare branches out over our deck. A gray squirrel sits on a branch on the south side of the linden. Motionless, its tail curled over its back, it is so still for so long that I fear it's been frozen stiff. But finally, it moves, washing its paws in its mouth, perhaps finishing off the taste of lunch. The squirrel doesn't hibernate, and it survives on seeds from the abundant supply of evergreen cones in our yard. Come spring, I find the chewed remains at the base of our trees where the squirrel has dropped them. As I watch, it dashes across to the spruce, and down, and is gone. Its movements are as sudden and rapid as blips on a computer screen, and I have often watched it darting effortlessly from one tree-top to another, high in the air.

The next day is nearly as cold, and in almost the same spot on the linden is a black-capped chickadee, its feathers plumped to the shape of a dark ball. It wears an elegant tuxedo plumage, a snow-white shirt, a steely gray waistcoat. I can see it breathing, and it moves its head from time to time, burying its tiny yellow beak in its feathers. The chickadee is a small miracle of evolution. It adjusts its metabolism in a sort of mini-hibernation to survive our subzero nights. It is also an excellent forager; other birds such as the titmouse and the nuthatch follow it around, knowing that where it goes there will be food. The chickadee sometimes stores food as squirrels do, and each year, in its minuscule brain it actually grows a new set of neurons, which some scientists believe allow it to remember where it has hidden caches of food for the winter season.

The chickadee may live as long as twelve years, but the size of its brain is too limited to hold on to twelve years worth of memories. Fernando Nottebohm of Rockefeller University in New York theorizes that the chickadee—along with many other songbirds, and a few mammals—grows new brain cells each year in order to store the new memories. The wild birds he has studied at the 1200 acres of Rockefeller University's Field Research Center in Millbrook, New York showed a peak of cell turnover in October, at the approach of winter's unequal hours. Humans seem unable to grow any new brain cells after trauma, stroke, or other disturbances destroy them. But perhaps we could learn something from the tiny chickadee.

If flight alone weren't enough cause for envy, we also know that birds can navigate without compass, sextant, or clock, sometimes traveling thousands of miles, often by starlight. What speeds them, and more important, what motivates them? What superordinary intelligence gives them sight and knowledge far beyond the range of our own poor senses, beyond the capacity of our own large, clumsy brains? Henry

Beston, watching birds migrate by night off the coast of Cape Cod, concluded, in his book called *The Outermost House:*

We need another and a wiser and perhaps a more mystical concept of animals. Remote from universal nature, and living by a complicated artifice, man in civilization surveys the creature through the glass of his knowledge and sees thereby a feather magnified and the whole image in distortion. We patronize them for their incompleteness, for their tragic fate of having taken form so far below ourselves. And therein we err, and greatly err. For the animal shall not be measured by man. In a world older and more complete than ours they move finished and complete, gifted with extensions of the senses we have lost or never attained, living by voices we shall never hear. They are not brethren, they are not underlings; they are other nations, caught with ourselves in the net of life and time, fellow prisoners of the splendour and travail of the earth.

In 1962, with the publication of Rachel Carson's book *Silent Spring*, a movement to limit the dangers of being caught in the net of life and time began. Carson's book continues to fuel protests against the use of pesticides, and surely no other book of its kind has had such a long legacy of truth, warning us of the price of using pesticides, to both birds and humans. But ornithologists now fear another kind of silent spring, one when the migrations of songbirds such as the wood thrush, the red-eyed vireo, and the Kentucky warbler are halted not by DDT but by loss of habitat. The songbirds that winter in Central and South America and fly north to us in spring are declining in numbers by 30 to 50 percent, according to the

North American Breeding Bird Survey, which monitors migratory bird populations along their routes for the U.S. Fish and Wildlife Service. Radar data from the National Weather Service, which normally watches tropical storms develop, confirm that since the publication of *Silent Spring*, bird migrations over the Gulf of Mexico have declined by 50 percent.

The answer is not in putting out more seeds in more bird feeders. The migrating birds need nesting places in woodland and forest habitats. Some songbirds require areas deep in a forest, and the increasing fragmentation of forest land by commercial development has made such places more and more difficult for the migrating birds to locate.

Instead of using only ornamental flowering shrubs, homeowners can plant more trees and use bushes that provide cover for birds and berries for them to eat. Holly, elderberry, shadbush, Juneberry, hackberry, firethorn, viburnum, and cottoneaster are all easy bushes to grow, providing food for birds and plantings for humans to enjoy as well.

The rapture of birdsong is something we take for granted, for it has no price in coin. "Songbirds make us better people," says Noel Grove in his book *Songbirds: Rhapsody in the Blue*. Birdsong simply serves to ease pain, better, I think, than many of the drugs sold to us by pharmaceutical companies. Perhaps John Keats was not exaggerating when he wrote of the nightingale:

Now more than ever seems it rich to die,
To cease upon the midnight with no pain,
while thou art pouring forth thy soul abroad
In such an ecstasy!

Of course, songbirds have not evolved for our benefit only, much as we would like to think so. Donald R. Strong, an ecologist at the University of California at Davis, believes that songbirds help to protect some deciduous trees by eating insects that would otherwise decimate the trees. Birds clean the trees of butterfly and moth eggs that would hatch into caterpillars, which would then munch on leaves. In such a sense, birds actually serve to provide pragmatists with an economic incentive for protecting them. The trees observed in Strong's experiments at the Tyson Research Center near Eureka, Missouri, were the valuable white oak, the tree Donald Peattie calls the "king of kings." The strong, straight wood of the white oak built great navies on both sides of the Atlantic. It is more resistant to rot than other types of oak, and it often outlives those who plant it.

The animals and plants of the places we inhabit have complex and sometimes little understood relationships, creating a delicate balance for the life and health of the entire planet. Allow one system to suffer, and others will soon be affected in what Chief Seattle described as "the web of life." In an oft-quoted letter to the U.S. government in 1852, Chief Seattle said: "This we know: the earth does not belong to man, man belongs to the earth. All things are connected like the blood that unites us all. Man did not weave the web of life, he is merely a strand in it. Whatever he does to the web, he does to himself." But whether or not birds provide jobs or investment opportunities, they give other beings something at least as valuable: birds provide a vision of power.

Flying above us, birds have been symbols of transcendence since time immemorial. Birds do effortlessly and mysteriously what we do only after centuries of effort, and then with frequent and tragic accidents. To fly as a bird flies is to be free of the body's prison and become immortal. Ancient Egyptian texts picture Ba, the bird of the soul, as a winged human hovering over the body of the deceased. The Egyptian god Horus is depicted with the head of a falcon. Vishnu, supreme god of creation to the Hindus, rides on Garuda, the eagle, and is sometimes portrayed as part man and part bird.

Birds were especially important to the Egyptian pantheon of deities. The ibis, a water bird with a long, curved beak, was worshiped as a symbol of creation. The ibis lays the world egg, and one creation story describes the world brought into being by the sound of the ibis's voice. From the cry of the ibis flew four gods and four goddesses who sang hymns to morning and evening to keep the sun on its course. Horus, a counterpart of the Greek Apollo, was a sun god with the head of a falcon. Seen soaring above, the falcon represented the sky, with one eye for the sun and the other for the moon. Horus vanquished his brother Set in the struggle between darkness and light, and became the ancestor of all the pharaohs and god of the sky. The ideogram depicting a falcon means "god" in ancient hieroglyphic texts. As incarnations of Horus, falcons were sacred and, unlike a simple totem, could not be hunted or eaten.

Messengers of divine will, the angels are nearly always portrayed with the wings of birds, gorgeous, iridescent wings of many colors, wings soft and white as an egret's, wings streaming golden rays of grace. Nike, god of Victory, has wings, and Eros, god of Love, and Hermes, courier to the gods. A dove sits on the Tree of Life. Holding the olive branch in its beak, the dove brought peace between man and God as the waters of the great flood receded. And when John baptized Jesus in the wilderness he saw "the Spirit descending from heaven like a dove, and it abode upon him."

Odin, as he walked through the wilderness, had two ravens, one perched on each shoulder, called Thought and Memory. He sent them out ahead of him to gather knowledge of the land. God commanded ravens to feed Elijah in the wilderness. The Inuit people regard the raven as sacred, for it will often lead them to prey. Ravens can grant wishes, answer prayers, and bring good luck.

The raven is a wild bird, but it follows societies of both animals and humans to find its food in the carrion left behind. It has acquired a reputation for portending death as a result. But its quick wits, curious eye, and dark, sleek beauty make it much admired, too. The pair of ravens living in our yard are the most curious of birds, their sharp eyes surveying whatever happens, their voices commenting in raspy report. Often, when I work outside, I see one of them perched not far away at the top of a tree, watching me and remarking on my presence with a few discreet squawks. I love to see them gliding slowly by overhead, silent, inky, and sleek as the stroke of the calligrapher's brush on silk.

Ravens, I know, form permanent pair bonds and hold a territory like this one, repairing and reusing a nest year-round. I have not seen their nest, however, nor have I seen any young. Perhaps this couple lives here without children as we do. Perhaps they will bring me thought, and memory, and a moment in the heart of the wild.

Primitive people believed in the power of animals to provide supernatural protection or loan special abilities. To walk as softly as a rabbit, run as swiftly as a deer, or hunt as well as an eagle, one could invoke the spirit of that animal through song or by wearing the creature's feathers or skin. Once, we thought of wild creatures as equal partners, if not superior to us many times over for their abilities to fly, to run, to see, and to hear much more than we could. At one time, a person in need of power would go on a vision quest, perhaps to a mountaintop, to fast, to pray, and to request a vision providing power in battle or the hunt. Sometimes the vision was one of wind, rain, thunder, or fire, a sign that the forces of nature would cooperate with you, blessing your efforts so that you could not fail. If the vision were of the spirit of a wild animal, you were greatly blessed, for to be visited by a wild creature who could fly through the air, swim in the waters, or dig into the earth was considered a great gift. Visions were brought back to the people, related in stories passed from one generation to the next and preserved for all to see in paintings on the walls of caves. Shared with others, these visions of power gave everyone the confidence to live in the world without fear.

Now we live not in caves but in cities and towns. We no longer seek success in the hunt or protection from mountain lions, but other gifts, more difficult to obtain: peace among nations, harmony in our families, personal wisdom, healing of psychological wounds. And we still look for visions of power in the wild.

We think of the wild as moving, creeping, stalking, flying, "running wild," yet to be wild is also to practice stillness. The great blue heron will stand still for so long, perched on the snag of a log or an outcropping of rock in a stream, that one must look very sharply at times just to see its cloud-backed plumage against the scenery. Smudged with color as softly as a watercolor, its feathers are gray, black, rust, and blue, the colors of stone, stream, and sky. Around its neck falls a ruff of streaming down; on its head a narrow comb is sleek and black. The heron's long, S-shaped neck holds up a head that often looks top-heavy with its elegant, long beak. As it stands in the stream, only its eye will be moving,

> watching a stone in water,
> A fish's hidden light.

The heron is also the most sensitive and shy of the waterfowl that visit the pond on our country property. Approaching the water from our cabin, we hear its high-pitched warning to other birds, and we are lucky if we catch a glimpse of it flying off before we get in sight of the water.

On a day in spring, I am walking to town on the bridge over the river when I catch sight of a heron standing on a rock upstream. I stop and stand unmoving, still and silent as it stands still and silent and unmoving on a stone, its glittering eye turned to me, offering me its moment of perfect stillness. Wind stirs the grasses on the riverbank, and water slips past me under the bridge. This is what it is like to be a tree, I think, to observe, and to know that what comes my way does not fear me because although I cast a shadow I do not stalk or kill. When one looks with a still mind, the separations of the ten thousand things cease to exist. The stone, the water, the tree, the heron, the sky, the sun, the shadows, and I, we all live in the heart of the wild.

Living with Trees

I will be standing in the woods
where the old trees
move only with the wind
and then with gravity.
WENDELL BERRY, "Stay Home"

My first glimpse of the world each day is through the branches of two trees outside my bedroom window, a spruce and a Scotch pine growing side by side. As dawn conquers darkness, their branches emerge silhouetted against the sky, and I can see their familiar shapes, the spruce as tall as our house and its companion the pine, a few feet shorter. They are like the two trees growing together in paradise. No doubt they were planted here many years ago to provide privacy, blocking the nearby neighbor's house from view. But they are much more than a fence. Their presence is reassuring, protective, tolerant. Winter or summer, they reach out and up, the branching boughs of the spruce with its small, stiff needles like neat rows of embroidery slanting toward the sky and the pine with its feathery clusters of needles that grow around the branches. I love the beauty of these trees, their presence, their self-sufficiency.

Our three-quarters of an acre of land is home to some thirty trees. The youngest is a red oak Bill found growing in the flower garden and transplanted to a sunny spot on the lawn. Protected by a cage of chicken wire, it's a little over a foot tall. Many of our trees look as if they were planted twenty years ago, when the house was built. These include a linden, a locust, six spruce, five Scotch pine, two maples, and two Douglas firs. They are home to many birds, squirrels, and insects. In June, when the linden blooms, bees cluster on its pale flowers, greedy for the spicy-sweet nectar. A white flowering dogwood and a weeping crab were planted for ornament in the courtyard. Cherry and apple trees have grown up wild.

A few of our trees are very old: two towering black willows and an old pear tree growing close to the house in the backyard. Our driveway curls around two stately ash left to stand, I am sure, by the original owner, in spite of the kink they make in the drive.

We all want to live with trees; a place without trees seems otherworldly. Trees hold the ground against erosion, provide shelter and shade, fuel, food, fabric, rope, and building material. Their sap gives us pitch, turpentine, rosin, and sugar; their bark gives us medicine. The very presence of trees is therapeutic. Studies have found that patients who have a view of trees from their hospital window heal faster after surgery and have less pain.

Our love of trees and the desire to protect them is something primal; perhaps we once lived in them, and our cells remember. As children, we climb trees, sit in them to feel tall, and build fantasy homes in them, mimicking the Swiss Family Robinson or Tarzan and Jane of story. Driving our county's roads in autumn, I often see an abandoned tree house in the bare branches of an ancient oak, on the edge of someone's property, a place for a child's secret house, a lookout where he or she was the world's master for a moment. Are we cherishing some racial memory of a time when we took sanctuary in the trees, naked and without fire, fleeing the faster predators who lived on the ground?

Or is it God we seek in the forest?

Given the close, if often unconscious symbiosis, the miraculous kinship between trees and humans, it is no wonder we have invested trees with divine powers. The first temples were sacred groves, the "high places" of pagan worship. Gods were thought to live in trees, which had roots reaching down into the sacred and mysterious underworld, gaining knowledge of the unseen. Thousands of years ago, as the Celtic people traversed Europe, it was the oak that endured, and the Celtic priests were called "druids," or "seers of oaks." The druids disdained temples built by men and chose instead the oak grove, where trees created silence and sanctuary imbued with the sacred life of the earth and the mother goddess. When we built sanctuaries of stone, we carved the columns to represent the trees of the first temples, scored them with lines to suggest bark, and topped them with capitals chiseled in leaf patterns.

Trees figure prominently in all religions. In Greece, oaks were sacred to the dryads, nymphs who danced in the oak groves to work their magic and protected trees from damage by mortals. In Norse legend, Yggdrasil, the sacred ash, grows from the underworld through the world of men and up into the realm of the gods, uniting the three worlds. Odin hung himself on the sacred ash just as Christ hung on the cross, a tree, and was reborn. Like Christ, he offered himself as a sacrifice, becoming the tree's fruit.

In Japan, those of the Shinto faith still deify the *kami* spirits of very large, very old, or very unusually shaped trees.

Tied with bits of string to mark them, they are protected from harm. The Japanese word for sacred place, *mori*, also means "grove."

The sacred pole of the Omaha was made from cottonwood, a tree imbued with mystical powers. Cottonwoods grow magically where no other trees can be found. Their roots seek out the tiniest trickle of water, and their small, flat leaves whisper music in the slightest breeze, sending messages to the gods on the sacred path of the wind. Many times, when I lived in the Southwest, I was grateful for the glimmering shade of a cottonwood tree in a desert canyon.

Cottonwood is also sacred to the Hopi, who for centuries have used its root for making their *tihu*, or kachina dolls. The kachinas represent supernatural beings from the parallel world of spirit who protect and assist human beings. They manifest in the forms of the natural world: clouds, rain, animals, birds, corn. The kachinas visit Hopi villages in winter and spring through the dancers who perform in ceremonies intended to ensure the people's health and that of the land, praying for the all-important and ever-scarce rainfall needed for fertile crops.

Because trees reach through earth and heaven and point to the sky, many cultures have worshiped trees and used them as symbols for the earth's axis. In ancient times, a huge evergreen tree stood outside the heathen temple at Uppsala in Sweden, representing Yggdrasil. In rural China, sacred trees stood at the entrance to villages. People believed that the spirits of the ancestors who once lived there resided in the sap of these trees. Buddha sat under a fig tree to obtain enlightenment. At the very center of paradise is the tree of eternal life, symbol of divine manifestation in nature. Like man, the tree is both spirit and matter, a symbol of both the fall and the redemption. The fir tree, because its leaves never die, became a symbol in Norse mythology for everlasting life. In his book *Sacred Trees*, Nathaniel Altman claims that woodsmen once refused to cut down firs because the trees were so holy, and fir trees that fell on their own were used to build churches.

Bill tells me that once, when the evergreen trees were not yet towering over our cabin as they do now, he set out on a December morning to cut down a Christmas tree for his children. Walking through a grove of Norway spruce with his ax in one hand, he sensed a consciousness in the fast-growing spruce which he himself had planted. Their will was powerful and proprietary in their relentless quest for light and space. The trunk of any one of them could have yielded to his ax, none being more than a foot in diameter at the ground, but he dared not touch them, majestically green and fragrant, the season's first snow at their feet. For one mad moment he believed the whole forest would rise up and overwhelm him if he did.

I too have known the will of a tree. I once felt less than friendly toward the old pear tree behind our house. It is a tall old tree, old even for a long-lived species, at thirty feet taller than any pear I'd seen. But it was much too close to the house, sometimes dropping a heavy, dead branch on the roof with a startling thud. The pear tree was a plume of snowy blossoms in April, when no other tree here blooms, but in June growing flowers in the yard was impossible in its shade, and one September, the pear delivered its final insult: a sea of hard, tasteless fruit that I spent days raking and hauling away. My sore muscles complained as I mumbled my plans for the tree's demise while raking up its useless fruit and hauling bushels of the stuff to the compost heap.

I could almost feel the pear tree's rage at the idea of being destroyed, as if it could read my mind. It had lived a long time, and it intended to keep on living.

Bill became the tree's ally and talked me out of chopping it down. The pear was a "forgiving" tree, he said, meaning one that would grow new branches wherever it was pruned. It could be topped off, trimmed of most of its branches, so the yard would have more sun, the house would be safe, and the tree would live.

I signed a treaty with the pear tree. In February, with Bill supervising, one young man with a hand saw and another with a chain saw up in the tree, the pear was given a good, noisy pruning while it stood quietly dormant. The cuts were sealed to prevent insects from infecting the wounds left by the saws. And sure enough, within a few months, the tree sent out eager new shoots reaching straight up to the sky. We chopped up the gnarled old branches cut from the tree for firewood and stacked it to dry. One morning, I burned some of the wood in our fireplace. The thick old bark of the pear tree resisted the flames and smoldered as if in defiance. The pear may be a forgiving tree, but it has not forgotten.

In the spring, a neighbor in the country calls to tell us that an ancient oak on the boundary of our property outside of town had fallen. No doubt he is thinking of cutting the wood. He has a truck and a chain saw and has cut fallen trees for us before. But it isn't until September, when the last of our summer guests are preparing to leave, that we decide to see the fallen tree for ourselves.

Bill's son Joe and his wife, Palma, walk with us up the steep hill behind the old farmhouse on our property. Palma carries her newborn, a daughter she has named Meryn. The two-month-old baby sleeps in Palma's arms. Bill and I carry walking sticks made of the branches of a fallen oak found the year before by our stream. The long, straight staves steady us as we follow the deer paths up the hill.

The season is changing from summer to fall, and a storm the night before has left the air cool and the sky full of clouds moving swiftly, like ships in full sail driven by an ocean breeze. A few clouds are still gray with rain. As we climb the hill, a brief shower anoints us, and we take shelter for a few moments under an apple tree. The hillside is dotted by these trees here and there—volunteers, Bill calls them, immigrants from the old orchard on the other side of the road. The young tree is full of fruit, apples blushing red on shiny green skin. Joe tastes an apple and pronounces it perfect for pies. We all taste the tart fruit, Bill and I discussing plans to come back with bushel baskets and ladders in a few weeks, after a frost has improved the fruit. The rain stops, and we continue up the hill, passing thickets of crab apple and tamarack.

At the top of the hill a grove of maple and ash borders a large meadow. Passing through the shadows, we seem now to be in another time, far removed from the machine age, a roving band of humans wandering the world. Wild blackberries still cling to the brambles, and small toads hop underfoot, alarmed at the noise we are making. As we come into the meadow, we catch sight of the white tail of a deer disappearing into the woods on the other side.

Sun comes out from behind the clouds to light the meadow blooming with the last flowers of summer: deep purple aster, goldenrod, wild yarrow, and milkweed. A drift of butter-flies passes through, gorgeous monarchs in their orange and black regalia, their wings edged with a pattern of white beads. They are bound for Mexico, twenty-five hundred miles to the south, where they will spend the winter. We follow them this way and that, attracted to their grace and beauty as they are drawn to the flowers in this meadow. They dance briefly for us and are gone as suddenly as they appeared.

Then we turn toward the dark woods at the western end of the meadow, the very edge of our property. Instantly, I spy the fallen giant, half in shadow, its long, broad, moss-covered trunk lying in state. We approach it slowly.

The trees here are mainly maple, and some are quite large. But this red oak once towered over them all. Its root mass is more than ten feet wide, wrenched from the ground and hanging with the serpentine ropes of its roots, still covered with clay, a twisted mass like the hair of a Medusa. This tree was never broken; it pulled itself right out of the ground, top-heavy, perhaps, with the weight of winter's snow and ice on its crown. What a spectacle it must have made, groaning and tilting, heaving its own roots from the earth, crashing down, shuddering to rest.

We judge it to be several hundred years old. It might have been a seedling when the War for Independence was won. It must have been tall when the Civil War was fought. Now it has fallen. I walk down along its broad trunk, measuring it to be over fifty feet long. Its bark is furrowed, covered by emerald mosses and the crenelated cups of celadon-colored lichens that grow here. A single brown leaf lies on the green moss. Stroking the velvety moss, my hand brushes the long threads of a spider's legs. It scurries off to hide under the fallen tree. With its tangle of branches and roots now on the ground, the old oak will be home to spiders and grubs, raccoons and rabbits. Already, deer have stripped bark from the smaller branches.

But when I touch the bare branch, I can almost feel a pulse, the beat of sap and cell, still living. Somehow, the fallen oak draws nutrients from the rain and the clay that clings to it roots. It might even sprout another tree somewhere, the old tree acting as a nurse. The ground is littered with its acorns.

Bill and Joe stand nearby, talking about the problem of getting trucks, chain saws, and planers up here. They're thinking of the wood, the long, straight-grained, sturdy wood of the oak, thinking of it cut, dried, planed, and polished, nailed into tables and chairs and bookshelves and cradles. To buy such wood at the lumberyard now is terribly expensive.

This time I am the one who argues for the tree.

"It's still alive," I say.

They turn to look at me, as I stand with my fingers on the tree's pulse. Bill nods. "It's true," he says. "It could still be alive."

"Then let it lie," I say. I want the tree to die here, rotting into the earth, dying the way only a tree can die, slowly, cell by cell entering into the life of other creatures around it, exchanging life for life, carbon for carbon. A great tree like this can die in a way we can only imagine, we who arrive on the planet screaming and depart complaining, with hardly a thought to what we leave behind, hardly a glimmer of understanding of the cycles giving life to the ten thousand things.

"It's beautiful, lying here," I say.

Bill argues for the wood. "But think of the beautiful things we could make from it and have in our home to look at every day." He jumps up on the fallen trunk to stand above me, gesturing. "Especially right here," he says, pointing, "where the grain would be so straight—"

"I want to look at it here. I'll come back to look at it here," I say. "This is where it belongs. Please, just leave it where it lies."

Palma nods, smiling, standing at the other end of the tree, holding her baby. Joe and Bill shrug, heads bowed for a moment in thought, and then they nod, too. Bill jumps down from the fallen oak and walks off with Joe to look at another tree.

Sanctuaries

In that moment of last clear light
when the world seems ready to speak its name,
meet me in the field alongside the pond . . .
JOHN DANIEL, "Ourselves"

Joe and Palma were married two years ago. A public ceremony took place on midsummer's eve, in the garden of the bride's home near Ann Arbor, Michigan. The night before, a violent storm blew down the marquee that had been set up in the garden. The next day, however, the sky was clear, and the marquee was raised up again, with tables and chairs arranged underneath for a banquet. There were the usual songs and speeches, feasting and flowers. Two families gathered to wish the couple well on their way through life and to celebrate the love they had found with each other.

But long before this, the couple had a private ceremony in a clearing by a stream on our country property. They came there to take their vows, exchange gold rings carved with oak leaves, and walk in the glade of trees Bill had planted twenty years ago. It was there and then, witnessed by oak trees and water rippling silver in the sun, that they say they felt truly married.

Many people find union in such places with the sacred, a union sometimes lacking for them in churches built of mortar and stone. They seek a religion of a different kind than that celebrated in our organized churches. By separating the church from the rest of the landscape, we have made the sacred place something we can ignore if we choose. But once, the sacred was everywhere: every landscape, every tree, every stream, and every rock was holy. Anne Bancroft, in her book *Origins of the Sacred*, explains our ancient spiritual connection with the landscape: "Once . . . the great human experiences were based on cosmic myths which operated in sacred time and space. They implied a deep sense of relationship with nature. The physical formations of rocks, trees, rivers and hills were luminous with meaning. The material world was seen as alive and beautiful and providing a sacred arena for human beings and their activities."

Our family's outdoor sanctuary is a hundred acres of woodlands and pasture near the house where Joe and his sisters grew up. Like much of the property in our county, it was once a dairy farm, with several barns and a herd of cattle, fields fenced by rambling roses, hills of oak, maple and white pine. Bill and Joe tore down one of the barns, using the wood to build a small cabin just uphill from the pond. Joe's sister Sarah and her husband, David, a carpenter, embellished the structure, adding a porch, finishing the inside walls, making closets for storage and counters for preparing food. Last summer, Bill's youngest daughter, Kate, and her fiancé, Jason, stayed at the cabin and built a screen door for the porch.

Maintaining this connection with home, even though the house they grew up in was sold during their parents' divorce many years ago, has created a bond of happy memories for this family, despite the very separate lives they now lead. Joe and Palma live in North Dakota, where Joe has found his first university teaching job, Kate and Jason are in Texas, Sarah and her family in the Hudson River valley north of New York City. Yet each of them manages to get to the cabin by the pond for at least a few days once a year, bringing Bill's grandchildren with them, and the little ones love the place as much as their parents do. The family story continues to be told here. It is a sacred place for us all.

The cabin is still about as rustic as a cabin can be. It smells of hay, straw, and milking as only old barn wood can. None of us live here year-round, yet we all come to this place for retreats of a few hours, a few days, a few weeks, or a few months. We are drawn to it to mark holidays, walking the dry brown fields on Thanksgiving Day, climbing the snowy hill above the stream at Christmas. Bill came here on his sixtieth birthday and in a private ritual of resurrection dug up some clay sculptures he had buried long ago. The heads of a man and a woman, with moss growing on their heads and dirt on their weathered faces, are now propped on the porch, gazing up the path that leads to the road.

We all have our favorite spots and even our favorite trees, markers of time and memory. In a small clearing beside the stream is a young oak Kate refers to as her tree, because she remembers it as a sapling, and she checks its growth each time she returns for a visit. It is now much taller than she, growing straight and healthy in a spot well away from the older trees. I don't know what would happen if she ever found it gone. Joe watches over the progress of two white oak trees he found last year growing on the hill above the stream. Their wood is valuable for the boats he dreams of building someday. Bill checks on the willows he planted to hold the bank of the stream against erosion in the torrents of spring. Their long, narrow leaves droop over the water and stir gracefully in the green shadows.

There are some trees that have not survived. In a clearing deep in the woods is the tall, straight trunk of a dead elm, a memorial to the blight which eliminated that noble tree from our lives. Shorn of its branches, bleached nearly white by the sun, it is now only a hollow pole, good for beehives and a perch for crows. The ground under it, so long in the shade of the great elm, is still clear of the thorn bushes and wild blackberry vines that overrun much of the wood. Once, I found there the outline, in some matted bits of fur, of a deer's carcass. Of the animal, nothing remained—even its bones had been carried away. But the impression of its body on the ground was clear. It looked as if the deer had simply lain down in that spot to die.

This summer we had a reunion, a joyful weekend of miraculously good weather when the family gathered for three days of swimming in the pond, walking in the woods, and sharing picnic meals. Old friends stopped by to say hello. Bill set up a camera and tripod for a series of family portraits and taught his three young grandsons to saw fallen logs for firewood. After a barbecue dinner on an August evening, we started a bonfire in a pit circled with stones outside the cabin. As sparks from the fire flew toward the sky, we pulled on shirts and sweaters and watched the sparks of the stars rising above us in the darkness. Palma held her infant daughter wrapped in a blanket in her lap. Gazing at the sky, we were each at peace in our own moment of silence, a still moment stitched securely between past and future, woven of our individual memories and dreams.

This place is our private sanctuary, but there are also public places preserved and protected for everyone who lives here. One such place is the eighty-one acre Moss Lake Nature Sanctuary at the northern end of the county, owned by the

Nature Conservancy. Moss Lake does not appear on road maps or tourism brochures, and there are no signs pointing the way. But it's not hard to find. It lies a few miles west of the town of Caneadea, off Route 243, down a dirt road just past one of the county's ubiquitous dairy farms. Looking down off the ridge of hill followed by the road, you see the lake sleeping below you. Passing a grove of hemlock, you come to a sign at the entrance to the site, which quietly but firmly proclaims the area off-limits to campers and sportsmen:

MOSS LAKE
NATURE SANCTUARY

This is an inviolate natural area where all living things both plant and animal are to be left undisturbed. If you will respect our regulations you are welcome to follow the foot path and enjoy the out of doors. Hunting, fishing, or trapping of wildlife, fires, smoking, camping or littering and the cutting, digging, or removing of trees, shrubs, or flowers are not permitted in this area.

NO PICKING OR COLLECTING

To the left of the sign is a large boulder carrying a brass plaque which tells a little more of the story:

MOSS LAKE BOG
has been designated a
Registered Natural Landmark

This site possesses exceptional value as an illustration of the nation's natural heritage and contributes to a better understanding of man's environment.

In *The Vascular Plants of Moss Lake Sanctuary*, a study of Moss Lake, Elizabeth Cook, who once taught biology at nearby Houghton College, begins to explain what is so special about Moss Lake: "The area has been of interest to botanists for many years because of its interesting rarities. Dr. Crystal Rork, late Professor of Botany at Houghton College, often took her students here. Miss Mabel James (1960) introduced the flora to her natural history classes from the Buffalo Museum of Sciences. Dr. and Mrs. Thomas Liston (1970) and Dr. and Mrs. R. Eliot Stauffer have studied and photographed the interesting plants."

Most interesting to profiteers at one time was the sphagnum moss that gave the lake its name. The fifteen acres of open water in Moss Lake are surrounded by a peat bog. The "peat exploiters," as Cook called them, dug channels through the bog to harvest the peat for sale to nurseries. The owners of the property, Mr. and Mrs. Orville Hotchkiss, also allowed botanists such as Crystal Rork and Mabel James to study the "interesting rarities" of plant life there. When Mr. and Mrs. Hotchkiss began to talk about selling the property, Mabel James was alarmed. She feared there was a very good chance that the peat exploiters would acquire the place and destroy the delicate balance of life in the bog by digging more channels and harvesting more and more of the peat.

In 1957, Mabel James launched a campaign to buy Moss Lake for the Nature Conservancy, engaging supporters and raising funds all over western New York. When she had raised enough money, and the Conservancy purchased Moss Lake in 1958, it acquired a new regional chapter in the bargain. The Western New York Chapter had organized expressly for the purpose of preserving the extraordinary environment of Moss Lake.

On a cool, breezy day in October, the sky over Moss Lake is slate blue and the water is beaten into scrolled patterns by the hand of the wind. It rains all morning as I drive north from my home in Wellsville, but by the time I park my truck in the picnic area, where there is space for a few automobiles, one picnic table, and up the hill, an old outhouse, the rain has stopped. Rain is now the only source for the water in the lake. But its origin is in ice. Some ten thousand years ago, a glacier scoured from the earth a fifteen-acre bowl, called by geologists a "kettle," and then filled it up with melting ice when the climate slowly warmed.

A narrow, muddy path curls through the woods and around the lake, unspoiled by signs, trash cans, railings, or any other evidence of building. The only item of construction is a large concrete slab blocking the way from the picnic area, to prevent vehicles from going any further on the trail. There isn't so much as a gum wrapper or a scrap of cellophane on the ground to indicate that anyone has been here—not an aluminum can or a cigarette butt anywhere in sight. I think of the many people who visit this place, especially in the summer just passed, and I'm proud to be among such a fastidious bunch. Here there is only the wind, the trees, the ferns, and the mosses growing in the shadows and the cool, pewter-colored water of the lake lapping against the shore.

In this brooding weather, Moss Lake has a mood so prehistoric that I would not be at all surprised to see a woolly mammoth sipping from the shallows. Archaeologists have found fragments of mammoth and mastodon bones in the peat, so we know that such creatures once roamed here.

On such a day, a wild symphony of wind plays in the trees. In the regal hemlocks it's a murmur in an indeterminate meter. In the oak, ash, birch, and maple that surround the picnic area, it's a strumming of soft, dry leaves, and in the white pine, it's a whispered recitative. The entrance to the preserve is shaded by large oak trees and fragrant white pine. In her monograph, Elizabeth Cook points out that one hundred years ago the area was referred to as "pine woods." The virgin pine was long ago felled for lumber like all the virgin forest in the Northeast. Then chestnut trees took over, succumbed to blight, and were finally replaced by oak. But left to its own devices, the woods repeat the old refrains, and the pine is coming back.

Lying deep in the cold shadows of hills piled up by the receding glacier, Moss Lake won't see spring until late in May. Then the place is home to wildflowers not often found growing elsewhere. Here you will see the tiny white and pink flowers of the trailing arbutus, now so rare a plant that it's a protected species. There are all kinds of violets: the marsh blue violet, the common blue violet, the sweet white violet, and the early yellow violet. White trillium grow under the pines, and near the water are blue flag iris, bloodroot, trout lilies, and lady's slippers. On the water near the shore drift scented white water lilies. In the meadows around the lake grow paintbrush, buttercup, yarrow, thistle, and milkweed. And in July, as Elizabeth Cook writes, "the bog appears as a wave of yellow," filled with sundews, a plant that traps insects for food and raises its innocent-looking yellow flowers to the sun.

There is no doubt that the most unique feature of Moss Lake, to those interested in biodiversity, is the "floating mats" of vegetation that have created the bog of sphagnum moss for which the lake is named. The mat of leather leaf shrub formed near the shore over a period of thousands of years, making a home for the moss, which likes the low mineral content of the rainwater in the lake. As the sphagnum died, it formed a peat bog under the mat, where oxygen-starved water retards decomposition, and the moss will not decay completely. Moss Lake is small enough so that its wave action is very gentle, and the peat bog settled in.

The environment of the lake is so unique that it has become home to many rare and unusual plants, and this qualified it for purchase by the Nature Conservancy. Unlike other conservation groups, which often expend resources lobbying for legislation, the Conservancy simply buys property with the objective of preserving the diversity of unique ecosystems or rare species of plants and animals.

On acquiring Moss Lake, the Conservancy built unobtrusive boardwalks out onto the largest of the lake's floating mats at the southeastern corner of the water to allow visitors a convenient observation deck and to prevent the curious from falling into the bog. All around the weathered boards grows *Sarracenia purpurea*, the purple pitcher plant, one of the most unusual of Moss Lake's unique bog vegetation. Shaped like a small jug, its curled, veined lip mottled purplish red, the pitcher plant, like the sundew, survives on the nitrogen-poor floating mat by trapping insects for food. The neck of the jug secretes nectar to attract bugs, and the lip is covered with tiny, down-pointing hairs that keep them from climbing out. After their last meal of nectar, the trapped bugs tumble down into the pool of rainwater waiting at the bottom of the jug and drown. An enzyme secreted by the plant digests them.

With protection from commercial development and with sufficient rainfall—more than adequate in this part of the world—a bog like this will remain just the way it is now for thousands of years. So the environment of Moss Lake is indeed a glimpse of a prehistoric wilderness. To a botanist like Jim Wolfe, who teaches biology at Houghton College, Moss Lake is a living classroom. Just as Mabel James, Crystal Rork, and Elizabeth Cook did before him, he brings his students here to learn the fundamentals of botany, and he occasionally gives guided tours.

Today he is preparing a large group of children who have poured out of yellow buses from the Buffalo area schools, making the picnic area suddenly noisy. They have made the two-hour trip with their science teachers, who stand among them looking a bit dazed from the ordeal. As the teachers try to quiet the children, Wolfe looks up at the sky suspiciously and pulls on a dark green waterproof parka. "I think it's going to rain," he says to me under his breath, looking around at the large group of children. I assure him that the rain has stopped and won't ruin our tour. He gives me a sidelong, skeptical glance. Wolfe has short, curly hair and impishly smiling eyes behind steel-framed glasses. He is dressed in a striped sweater and pressed pants, as if he just came from the classroom, except for the addition of practical, lace-up waterproof boots.

"My name is Wolfe, just like the animal," he tells the children and, throwing back his head, gives a quick wolf howl, looks around, and grins. That gets everyone's attention, for the moment at least. Wolfe explains the meaning of a nature sanctuary, telling the class, "Nothing comes in, and nothing goes out," he says. "And these," he adds, holding up one of the mysterious pieces of dry bread now being passed around by the teachers, "are your admission tickets."

Wolfe also warns the children about playing in the water

by relating the story of the body found in a peat bog like this one in England. The "bog man" discovered in 1984 was dubbed "Pete Moss" by the British press. Pete was the victim of ritual sacrifice about 50 A.D. on Beltane, the first day of May, one of the important "cross-quarter" days between the solstice and the equinox celebrated by the ancient Celts. Pete was given a breakfast of Beltane cake—a burned pancake— after "winning" a ritual lottery. Following his murder, he was tossed into the bog as a gift to the Celtic god Bel.

In the cold, acidic waters of the British bogs, many such bodies—male and female—have been found. In a bog, where there is little oxygen, flesh cannot easily decompose. Such oxygen-starved waters are not good homes for nibbling fish or other hungry animals. So the bodies of these ancient people are sometimes found fully fleshed, even with hair, clothing, and braided cords intact around their necks.

The ropes found with some of the bog men were used to strangle them. Then, like Pete Moss, their throats were cut and their skulls bludgeoned with an ax. When Wolfe finishes his gruesome story of the bog man's murder, his audience of children falls silent, obviously impressed. Then there is flock of fluttering hands and a chorus of questions: "Why? Why did they kill him?" they cry. "What for?"

Wolfe tries to explain. "These people thought they had to do this to make their gods happy."

The children consider this information for a moment, and their teachers remind them that their fate could be similar to that of Pete Moss if they go too near the water.

Now that he's got everyone's attention, Wolfe embarks on his natural history tour in a lighter vein. "I want you to use all your senses today," he tells the children. "Use your eyes, and your ears, and your noses. You can look at things and smell things and touch things, but don't pick anything. I might pick a leaf to show you what it is, but I don't want anyone else to pick anything." True to his word, he bends down and picks a leaf growing close to the ground as the children follow him up the path. He breaks the leaf in half and holds it under the eager twelve-year-old noses for them to smell, asking the children what it reminds them of. Some say mint, some lemon. My nose recognizes the fresh scent of wintergreen. It is only one of the 264 species of plants Elizabeth Cook cataloged in the area. We walk further down the path, and before we even get to the lake, the children also learn about mosses, ferns, and lichens. Wolfe explains that the smooth, round rocks littering the path near the shore were shaped by the same glacier that made the lake. As he stands on the path, a dragonfly hovers near him and he captures it in his hand for a moment, holding it carefully by its wings to show the children its abdomen, its thorax, and its bulging eyes. He assures us the beautiful creature will not sting and then releases it to fly away. Twenty pairs of young eyes follow it as it floats off into the forest.

At the shore of the lake, everyone joins in the Moss Lake ritual of feeding our pieces of dry bread to the catfish that live in the lake. Someone stocked the lake years ago, and while the small, bewhiskered fish have not exactly thrived in the poorly oxygenated water, they have certainly multiplied, kept alive in part by frequent meals of dried bread thrown them by visitors. They nose toward our gifts, mouthing the torn bits of bread and ducking back into the murky water. Fragrant sweet fern grows by the shore, and Wolfe picks a small piece for the children to sniff before we head back up the path.

After a short trek along the muddy path in the shadow of tall hemlocks, we approach the boardwalk and the floating mat, where dried white heads of cotton grass hover like white-winged moths, dancing in the breeze. As we file out onto the boardwalk, Wolfe pulls up a piece of dripping moss and shows it to the children. Squeezing out the water, he explains that native people used the moss for baby diapers, because it is so absorbent, and for binding wounds, because it also has antibiotic properties. He has the good taste not to mention menstrual pads, which I know were another application of the moss. I have also read that scientists are now studying the biodegradable moss for use in absorbent pads, which would be less of a burden to landfills as are the millions of disposable diapers being discarded today.

Gathering the class around him on the boardwalk, Wolfe picks one of the pitcher plants to let the class see the flies floating dead in a pool of rainwater. He points out the few white pines struggling to grow on the floating mat, looking sickly from lack of the nitrogen the pitcher plants get from the flies. He shows us the cranberries that grow in the bog and the blueberry bushes, which still hold a few purplish berries. By now it is clear that this place is much richer in plant life than most of us have seen before. Creation has stitched here for eons, and we are observing the tapestry of variety that can result when the world weaves freely.

As we follow the path around the lake, Wolfe stops now and then to talk about hemlocks and oak galls and the fungus that grows on the old trees. A damp wind stings our cheeks as we walk silently single file down the last narrow curve of the trail around the lake. Ending up once again at the picnic area, the children noisily devour lunch from sacks brought out of the buses. Prompted by their teachers, they gather to thank Wolfe. He smiles, his eyes bright behind his steel-rimmed spectacles, and waves cheerfully from the window of his car as he drives away.

After the last child has run down the path to board a yellow school bus and the bus has lumbered off down the road, the woods around the lake sigh deeply, alone again in an ice-age reverie. Now the mosses will die and sink into layers of peat as they have for a thousand years. Year after year, the trees will give their leaves to the soil, and the soil will give nourishment to the trees. Rain will fill the lake, and ice will grow on it as it waits for spring.

A gust of wind moves water toward the shore, stirs acorns to drop from the oaks, and sends brown leaves flying toward winter. I listen to the wind in the trees singing Moss Lake to sleep, to dream of tomorrow, another age away.

Riding the Wind

You make the clouds your chariot
and ride on the wings of the wind.
Psalm 104

We cannot see the wind, but we can see its influence. Clouds shift in shape and position minute by minute, blown by the wind. Trees are bent by constant wind into tortured forms. Ripples on water and sand show wind's sculpting hand. Wind makes colored pennants fly and sets the stars and stripes of our flag streaming. (When astronauts landed on the moon, where there is no atmosphere and as a result no wind, the flag had to be wired to keep it from drooping.) Wind transports the seeds of dandelions, milkweed, and thistles. It pollinates the wheat used in our bread. It sends spores and even some spiders on their way through the world. Hawks will circle a canyon, lifted by spirals of rising warm air currents, wings outstretched and still, riding the wind, just for fun.

Today as I work by an open window I hear trees rustling with the wind's music. Emily Dickinson called it

> . . . that old measure in the boughs,
> That phraseless melody
> The wind does, working like a hand
> Whose fingers brush the sky.

I leave my windows open to let the wind come in. With each great gust I hear it slamming shut doors all over the house and then opening them again, like an uninvited guest.

No other element is called by so many names. A zephyr is a sweet-scented breeze from the west, named after Zephyrus, the son of Eos the dawn, and Astraeus, the starry sky. A chinook roars down the slopes of the Rockies, sending temperatures plummeting twenty to thirty degrees in minutes. In Alaska, they call it a williwaw. A warm, dry wind off the slopes of the Alps is called a foehn. A monsoon brings rain from tropical seas. A squall is a sudden rise in the wind, dangerous to sailboats on the open sea. In Russia, a winter wind that drives snow already on the ground into a frenzied blizzard is called a purga.

The simoom sends blinding dust storms across the Sahara. The romantic Mediterranean mistral blows cold winds into southern France and is said to stir up trouble, too. The sultry sirocco, like California's Santa Ana wind, is accused of causing madness, mayhem, and even murder. Unlike the soft winds that stir melodies in trees and ripples on a pond, these winds make us lose our grip and come unhinged. Telling the story of a murder in southern California in "Some Dreamers of the Golden Dream," Joan Didion implies that the Santa Ana winds could be an accessory to the crime: "October is the bad month for the wind, the month when breathing is difficult and the hills blaze up spontaneously. There has been no rain since April. Every voice seems a scream. It is the season of suicide and divorce and prickly dread, wherever the wind blows."

The winds blowing across the Atlantic sent sailing ships to trade for spices and gold and became known as the trade winds. At the equator, where the winds die and leave the ship becalmed, they became known as the dreaded doldrums. In 1805, Sir Francis Beaufort, a rear admiral in the British navy, devised a scale for sailors to identify wind force by simply looking at the wind's effect on the sea. When the wind is calm, the sea is like a glassy mirror. A light air of one to three knots on Beaufort's scale makes large wavelets with breaking crests and a few whitecaps. A gale of thirty-four to forty knots will make wave crest edges break into spray, and a storm of forty-eight to fifty-five knots will cause very high waves with overhanging crests. In a hurricane, the air is filled with foam and the sea is white with spray.

When aircraft climbed high into the earth's atmosphere, we discovered new kinds of winds. Moving as fast as two hundred miles per hour in ribbons sixty miles wide and three thousand miles long, the jet streams affect our weather by bringing cold air from the poles. In the summer of 1992, the polar jet stream dipped down and flung a lasso of cold air across the United States, bringing rain wherever it collided with warmer air from the south. It was the region's coldest July on record, averaging only 71.7 degrees Fahrenheit, 2.3 degrees cooler than normal. Eight states—Iowa, Maine, Massachusetts, Michigan, Minnesota, Nebraska, New York, and Wisconsin—reported their coldest July temperatures ever. Meteorologists speculated that the jet stream might have been displaced by the eruption of Mount Pinatubo in the Philippines the year before.

In the troposphere, the layer of air that extends ten miles above the surface of the earth, wind is always in motion, exchanging hot air with heavier, cooler air turning in rotation with the earth. The bigger the differences in pressure, the stronger the wind. The wind blows most violently during a storm, and when updrafts are blown into a churning vortex, the "twister" of wind we call a tornado is the result. The wind in a tornado can blow up to three hundred miles an hour and cause anything it touches to explode. By sucking up air into its funnel from around a building, the tornado causes a sudden drop in pressure outside the structure. Inside, the pressure builds up and pushes out windows and walls.

The closest I have come to a tornado was on a Memorial Day weekend in 1985, when I lived in a small town in Pennsylvania. On the evening of May 31, I went to the home of some friends for a picnic. A rainstorm forced the party indoors, while the host grilled hot dogs and hamburgers on a sheltered porch. We were all having such a fine time that we only laughed when the house shook with the wind and the lights blinked on and off.

The next morning turned out to be sunny, and I went for a drive on roads littered with broken tree limbs. In a few places, I was surprised to see large, fallen tree trunks almost blocking the road. In fact, several tornadoes had touched down in the nearby town of Kane the night before. One of the twisters picked the roof up off the high school and set it down again slightly askew. I discovered later that one of my students survived by crawling under his kitchen table while the storm blew out all the windows in his home. When he ventured from his shelter, he saw shards of glass from his front window embedded in the wall across from it, launched like deadly arrows. It took a good year for the shock of the experience to wear off; writing an exquisitely descriptive account of the demonic wind helped him exorcise the memory.

Every summer, the National Hurricane Center tracks between sixty and seventy tropical storms that have the potential to become hurricanes, winds which form a spiral that acts, as physicist James Trefil describes it, like a vacuum cleaner, sucking up moist air on the ocean's surface. A calm eye forms at the center of the vortex, and once the winds reach a speed of seventy-five miles per hour, the storm is officially declared a hurricane and given a name, starting with "A" and working down the alphabet as the season progresses. In his book *Meditations at Sunset: A Scientist Looks at the Sky*, Trefil expresses his disappointment that there has never been a Hurricane Zelda because the season never produces enough storms to reach the letter "Z." Once, the names were all female: killer storms like Agnes, Betty, Cleo, and Camille. Today, we give hurricanes both male and female names. Hurricane Andrew, in August 1992, has been called the nation's costliest disaster, causing over $30 billion worth of damage and leaving a quarter of a million people homeless. People and animals alike were traumatized by the wind that came in the night. Lions roared in their cages at the Dade County Zoo, and monkeys trembled for days. For months afterward, children feared the sound of wind and rain and suffered from nightmares and depression—some even attempted suicide.

In September, the Hawaiian island of Kauai was blasted by Hurricane Iniki, a name that means "piercing as pangs of wind or love."

Gods of the wind are powerful figures in most mythologies. In native myth and ritual, wind brings vision and authority; the Pueblo call it the breath of the land. God spoke to Job out of the whirlwind, and Ezekiel's vision came to him in a whirlwind blowing from the north. Black Elk's vision came to him with "a cleansing white wind from the north." Rudra, god of storms in Hindu myth, is an archer whose arrows bring the transformation of death.

But wind isn't always a menace. Aeolus, Greek god of the winds, ruled wind instruments like the flute and gave his name to the Aeolian harp, a musical instrument with strings played by the wind. It is said that King David had a similar instrument which he hung over his bed at night, soothing him to sleep with music made by a midnight breeze.

In Norman, Oklahoma, the University of Oklahoma's College of Fine Arts honors wind at a Summer Wind Festival with chamber music concerts and a kite design competition. The wind festival's logo is a circle studded with rays to depict the sun and inside it a wheel with four spokes swirling in motion: the four winds. This symbol of the four winds is found on the pottery, jewelry, and ceremonial costumes of native peoples, who knew that the sun and the spinning world made wind and that wind, like breath, brought life.

In Holland, a country that always brings to mind images of picturesque windmills, energy gathered from the wind once ran the prosperous factories for sawing lumber and weaving cloth. Wind pumped water wells on isolated farms across the midwestern United States in the nineteenth century, and now "wind farmers" in our western states use wind-powered turbines to produce a clean form of electricity. In one year, wind generators cut carbon dioxide emissions by 2.7 billion pounds in California alone. Many other states—thirty-six of them, according to the U.S. Department of Energy—are capable of using the wind to make electric power. European nations have plans to convert many homes and businesses to wind power by the year 2000.

Where wind is regularly available, even a small home

can use a windmill. Some are portable and weigh only twenty pounds, ideal for camping. Residential windmills can be mounted on two-inch pipes and will produce energy to match the utility company's output in wind as light as 7.5 miles per hour. They can power refrigerators, lights, televisions, and other appliances for the home.

Wind was also once a form of transportation. For well over a hundred years—until the Wright brothers flew at Kitty Hawk in 1903—hot air balloons riding the wind were the most common form of aircraft in America. Frenchman Jean-Pierre-François Blanchard made the first balloon flight in America on January 9, 1793, in Philadelphia. Accompanied by a little black dog, he flew fifteen miles from the Walnut Street prison yard to what is now Deptford, New Jersey. "What sweet ecstasies take possession of the soul of a mortal who, leaving the terrestrial abode, soars into the ethereal regions!" he said of riding the wind.

In the 1960s the availability of new synthetic fabrics and propane fuel systems made ballooning easier and more economical than before. The craze for hot air balloons was reflected in Jimmy Webb's popular song, "Up, Up, and Away!" Today, there are approximately six thousand hot air balloons certified by the Federal Aviation Administration (FAA) in the United States alone. All over the United States, from May to October, people are enchanted with the sight of colorful hot air balloons.

In the town where I live, balloon fever strikes every year on a weekend in July during the Great Wellsville Balloon Rally. The Balloon Rally Store sells official Great Wellsville Balloon Rally T-shirts, sweatshirts, hats, pins, and posters. Local artist Tom O'Grady designs a new poster every year for the rally, showing balloons against the backdrop of a local landmark. In 1993, for the eighteenth annual rally, O'Grady's poster depicted balloons drifting by Wellsville's town hall. I remember this scene from last year's rally, when, after a weekend of steady rain, the balloons took flight, floating low over Main Street on Sunday morning after the rain finally stopped.

At Bartholomew's Gift Shop, you can buy balloon coffee mugs, balloon beer mugs, balloon jewelry, balloon ash trays, balloon key rings, stained glass balloon sun-catchers, balloon mobiles, and paper lanterns in the shape of balloons. Vans, trucks, and trailers carrying the wicker balloon gondolas and sporting signs advertising balloon rides appear in the parking lots of shopping centers and motels. Balloons of paper and plastic are displayed in store windows, along with signs on the days of the rally saying, "When balloons go up, our prices go down!"

Businesses raffle off tickets for a free ride in one of the balloons. A ride can be had at a price from the owners of balloons with such names as Sky Turkey, Pink Lady, Magic Sky, Topper, Rainbow Chaser, and Reverie, but space on the flights fills up fast. This year, I've arranged ahead of time to join a flight on a balloon called High Hopes. High Hopes is sponsored by Northern Lights Candles, a company owned by my neighbor Andy Glanzman. He has recommended High Hopes and its pilot, Greg Livadas of Rochester.

Flying in a hot air balloon is great fun, but piloting one is certainly not all fun and games. To keep a license to fly, balloon pilots must undertake ground school training, pass examinations conducted by the FAA, fly check rides with instructors, put in at least ten hours of flight instruction—including a solo flight—and attend safety seminars.

Today's hot air balloons are inflated with air heated by propane burners controlled by the pilot. In Wellsville, we often hear the hiss of propane burners blasting the balloons with hot air to keep them aloft even before we see the balloons themselves drifting by. The colorful envelopes are made of taffeta-weave, rip-stop nylon, coated to protect it from the elements, and they often bear the logo of a sponsor. They expand with the heated air, which becomes lighter than surrounding air as its molecules spread out from one another. Once lighter than air, the balloon floats up and rides the wind. Each balloon is as big as a house, and seeing a flock of them floating among the clouds is like watching a surrealist painting come alive. I sometimes see the blue and white Carpet Town balloon sail right past my window. The carpet and furniture store is just a mile away; the pilots take off from the store's parking lot and ride the wind down the river near my home.

Inflating the envelope with air warmer than that surrounding the balloon is easiest in early morning and early evening, when the atmosphere is cool, so most balloon flights take place at those times. Wind is usually gentlest at these times, too. Pilots avoid the stronger winds in the middle of the day, and flying in hot weather is particularly difficult. At this year's pilot's briefing, Marion W. Lunneman of Webster, New York, whose balloon Pink Lady bears a big initial "L" in pink, said she had a close call the previous weekend. She had to cut a flight short and make a precipitous landing in a parking lot after nearly running out of propane just trying to keep her balloon aloft in the heat. Happily, the temperature has cooled off this week, and the skies are clear.

A balloonmeister at the Great Wellsville Balloon rally obtains weather reports, briefs the pilots on conditions before each launch, and gives the okay to fly. The weather is better some years than others. This year the Friday night launch is canceled because of gusting winds that could make for difficult and dangerous flights. The disappointed crowd of hundreds mills around, watching children fly kites that swirl about in the roller coaster winds. One kite is decorated with the bold profile of the space shuttle, white against a field of dark blue.

I pass the time talking with Greg Livadas, who is tall and broad-shouldered and has straight brown hair that falls over his ears. Sitting on the tailgate of his truck, he wears acid-washed jeans and a navy blue knit polo shirt, pinned with his light blue official balloon rally identification badge. His red and white Ford pickup has a hydraulic lift on the back for picking up his balloon's 250 pounds of envelope fabric once it is stuffed into a large canvas duffel bag. The truck's license plate reads "UpUpAway."

Working as a journalist in Rochester during the week, Livadas runs a weekend business with his balloon, taking passengers on joy rides or doing promotions for businesses like Glanzman's Northern Lights Candles. He tells me he had his own first flight in a balloon at the age of sixteen, winning the ride in a raffle. He was hooked on the spot with the excitement of flight and got his pilot's license and his first balloon not long afterward.

Livadas enjoys sharing the pleasure of riding the winds with first-time flyers. "I like to ask people when they're getting in the balloon, 'Is this your first time in a balloon?'" he says. "When they say yes, I say, 'Me, too!'" Actually, he's a veteran, with fifteen years experience as a pilot and some five hundred flights to his credit. Balloon rides are a popular gift for the person who has everything, and Livadas has sometimes taken newlyweds or those celebrating a graduation or an anniversary for surprise rides. A college friend of Livadas proposed marriage while on a High Hopes flight, presenting the young lady with a diamond ring he had hidden in his sock. Apparently she was too overwhelmed to refuse. No doubt that's what he was counting on.

Livadas uses his hands as he talks, one hand over the other, pointing in opposite directions, to show me how the wind blows in layers, one direction close to the ground and another higher up. Describing the wind blowing down off the surrounding hills and through this river valley, his hands tilt toward one another in a V, palms down, index fingers almost touching. He draws a box in the air to describe the wind currents shaped by five-thousand-foot-high mountains in Albuquerque, New Mexico, where balloon pilots can sometimes go up and make ninety-degree turns in the air by riding the wind.

By Saturday morning of the rally, the winds have died down, and forty-four balloonists gather at dawn for the scheduled 6:30 A.M. launch. The concession stands which sell balloon paraphernalia and hot dogs are still boarded up. On both sides of a dike in Island Park, on the banks of the Genesee River, the wicker balloon gondolas lie on their sides, attached to the limp envelopes spread out in front of them. The baskets make lightweight and flexible platforms for landing, and are shielded top and bottom with brown suede trim to protect the wicker from wear and tear. Each balloon needs a crew of three or four people to assist with inflation, and a chase vehicle to follow and retrieve the balloon when the flight is over. The High Hopes crew of two men and two women sip coffee and yawn while Livadas attends the pilot's briefing. Most of Wellsville is still asleep, but while we're waiting, a few dozen balloon enthusiasts drift in to watch the launch, many carrying cameras and camcorders along with thermoses of coffee.

At 6:15, balloonmeister James Willauer, who also pilots a balloon called Top Gun, gives the pilots the okay to fly. He announces the morning's race, a "key grab" of a key that has been tied to a flagpole at the Wellsville airport, over a hill to the north. The balloonist who maneuvers close enough to grab the key will win $1,000. The winds at low elevations, he says, are to the south, in the general direction of the Genesee, but climbing to higher elevations the pilots may find a northbound breeze. Winds are gentle, at two to three miles per hour, the sky is clear, and the temperature is moderate at 64 degrees. It's perfect weather for flying. "Have fun, and be careful up there," is the last word from Willauer. The pilots hurry off to their balloons. Livadas strides briskly up to High Hopes, wearing a lightweight blue jacket over his blue shirt, and without a word begins his equipment check.

Each balloon has a large, motorized fan nearby for blowing cold air into the envelope. Livadas cranks up the fan and circles his balloon as his crew hold the mouth of the balloon open with the fan blowing in. The noisy fans whir and sputter all around us, and in moments the balloons swell voluptuously, heaving up from the ground like colorful hump-backed whales. As the High Hopes envelope fills, showing its vertical rainbow stripes against a black background, Livadas checks it for leaks, fluffing the nylon. Then he hooks up the tanks of propane to his double burners and checks them, too, kneeling in the gondola as it lies sideways on the ground. When he has sent a few golden jets of flame puffing hot air into its envelope, the eight-story-high balloon tilts upright, clearing the ground, and Livadas stands up in the gondola. Along with Jamie Sherwood, a young woman with very long, curly hair who has won the Northern Lights raffle for a balloon ride, I swing my legs over the side of the gondola and step inside. The High Hopes gondola will hold four, and we're waiting for one more passenger. All around, other balloons fill the sky, and the morning crowd has grown to what looks like several hundred. One by one, the motorized fans fall silent, replaced by the periodic hiss of propane burners.

Just in time, a tan-colored Mercedes station wagon pulls up on the dike, and Andy Glanzman gets out, carrying a camcorder to record the flight. Looking sleepy, Glanzman climbs into the basket and accepts a kiss from his wife, Tina, who will chase High Hopes in her station wagon along with the ground crew in the truck. She waits to see us take off along with the couple's two children, eight-year-old Silka and nine-month-old baby Tony, who sits in a stroller and gazes up wide-eyed at the towering balloon.

In a few moments, the balloons around us start to rise into the air, to the delight of the crowd. One of the first to take flight is Sky Turkey, a familiar blue balloon emblazoned with a red, white, and yellow cartoon figure of a bird that looks a lot more like a chicken than a turkey. With eager pilots taking balloons up all around us, there's a bit of a traffic jam, and we wait as Livadas blasts hot air into the balloon to keep it upright until the space above us is clear, while Glanzman films the others taking off. When we see an opening, Livadas gives the balloon a few more blasts of hot air, and we soar smoothly several hundred feet up from the ground, waving to the smiling, upturned faces of the people below.

Livadas wants to follow the river, so he stays at this height, where the wind blows south. Balloon pilots are at the mercy of the wind, but they can plan for it with information from the weather service and watch for it in the motion of clouds, smoke, or flags unfurled in the breeze. High Hopes is also equipped with a gauge attached to a sensor high on the envelope to measure the balloon's temperature, an altimeter giving the balloon's height, and another gauge measuring its rate of ascent, as well as a hand-held radio for communicating with the ground crew. In our fifty-minute flight, he used the radio to talk to the crew following us in the truck, but the only gauges I saw him watching were the ones on the twin tanks of propane fuel tucked down in either side of the gondola. Without sufficient fuel to keep the envelope full of hot air, the balloon would quickly descend. The two tanks hold a total of forty gallons, and Livadas likes to use no more than half for any given flight. He leans on the side of the gondola with one hand on the propane valve for most of the flight.

As we drift away from the launch site, we can see the Carpet Town balloon doing tricks for the spectators already leaving the park via a footbridge across the river. The blue and white balloon descends slowly in front of the bridge until the basket nearly touches the water, then goes up again. The up and down movement is the easiest for a pilot to control, since elevation is purely a matter of how much hot air he allows into the envelope.

We fall silent as the balloon climbs higher. The sounds of

traffic and machinery so common in the background of consciousness most of the time are gone. The only sound is the blast of the propane burners triggered by the pilot at regular intervals of twenty or thirty seconds. Riding the wind, we can no longer feel the wind or hear it. We're a thousand feet high, at eye level with the sun streaking green hilltops gold. White scarves of morning mist stream through the valleys below. We float free of the earth, suspended in a little eternity. It is as if we are flying with the soul in the moment between inhalation and exhalation practiced in yoga, a moment called *kumbhaka*, "the full vessel." It is this freedom and the accompanying euphoria the balloonist craves. Flying a balloon is not so much about getting somewhere as about being somewhere, being at one with the wind.

"It's just like a dream," Glanzman says softly. We have all had dreams of flying, seeing the round tops of trees and the roofs of houses from above, as a bird would, transcending space and time. Livadas tells us of a dream he's had of flying in the gondola without the balloon above him.

Leaving the launch site behind, we move south over farmland that begins to draw straight rows of corn into fields and blocks of pasture on one side of the river, where the land is flat. A herd of cows runs from the sight of us, lowing with surprise. Drifting slowly over green pasture and blue water with the sun behind us, we see the shadows made by the balloons around us, fat exclamation points against the treetops, and occasionally, the colorful splash of a balloon's reflection in the river below. The other balloons drift along like huge, floating Easter eggs painted in gorgeous designs. Two other balloons are nearby, following the same current of wind we ride. One is blue with yellow stripes and a red zigzag across its middle, adorned with yellow pennants, and the other is blue with a horizontal stripe of multicolored squares. We wave to the other balloons and call to them when they're close enough. "How's the weather, Paul?" Livadas yells to the pilot of the blue and yellow balloon.

After talking to balloon pilots, I have come to the conclusion that unlike most of us, they do see the wind. They judge what they know is typical about the wind, how it is influenced by hills, rivers, fields, and other features of the landscape— even the man-made ones like buildings—and, of course, the weather. Watching the signs in the microclimate around them as they fly, they can pick up a current of wind and travel it as someone in an automobile would turn onto one road or another on the ground. They look at the sky and see not an empty space but a living map of the wind.

Besides watching the wind, balloon pilots are always on the lookout for a likely landing spot. Livadas says he's landed in all kinds of places, "from fields just sprayed with manure to cemeteries, to a backyard where someone was having a graduation party." The High Hopes chase truck has followed us, visible below on a road running parallel to the river. Livadas checks in on the radio, describing a field he sees just beyond a curve in the river, with a house nearby. The crew will be responsible for getting permission from the owners to land. As we draw closer, we can see that there's a dirt road coming right back to the field. "This looks like the spot," he says, nodding. There are no telephone poles with dangerous wires to negotiate nearby, no tall structures to dodge. The field looks flat, dry, and long enough for the envelope of the balloon to stretch out on the ground when it is deflated.

As we cross the water, a great blue heron flaps by and perches in a tree to watch.

The balloon drifts diagonally toward its landing spot as Livadas lets the air in the envelope cool and grow heavy. Then, he pulls a cord, which opens a vent above, cooling the air in the envelope even more and allowing the balloon to drop slowly toward the ground as he brakes it with a few short blasts of hot air.

We come gently to a stop, floating inches above the ground, where dew still sparkles in the morning sun. We compliment our pilot on his skill, and he only shrugs. "It's all in the wind," he says, smiling.

About Color

Stand in the sun long enough to remember
that nothing is made without light.
MARGARET GIBSON, "Radiation"

I often wake in the hour just before dawn. Outside is an ambient light, one that seems exhaled from the heart of things, like an odor. At first, the trees outside my window are an etching in black and white. But on the horizon is a smudge of gold, bringing light and blue to the sky. As the light grows, I can see that the boughs of the spruce trees are dark green, and their brown bark has patches the color of salmon, umber, and verdigris.

Color is light. Light waves reflect from the surfaces of things, and depending on which are absorbed and which bounced to our eyes, we see a certain color. An object absorbs some light waves and scatters others depending on its structure and its pigmentation. In the last century, John Tyndall, an English physicist, discovered that the sky is blue because minute dust particles in the atmosphere scatter the wavelengths at the blue end of the spectrum. If not for the dust, we might see the black backdrop of space. The same is true of blue eyes. The "blue" iris has many unpigmented cells which scatter the blue wave lengths. And snow is white because the many spaces between snow crystals separate the light and scatter it about to such an extent that the colors all run together.

Today as I sat reading, I saw a rainbow shine suddenly for a moment on my hand as it held the book. A shaft of light bent at just the right angle through a window ornament, a lovely thing given me by Bill's youngest daughter, Kate. There on my skin, as if a blessing, were bands of red, orange, yellow, green, blue, indigo, and violet. The violet was especially bright, perhaps because I have lavender tones in my skin. How wonderful, I thought, if we could wear a rainbow!

And with those seven notes, what a symphony of color we see: scarlet, cinnabar, vermilion, rouge, ocher, gold, lemon, and saffron, emerald, celadon, turquoise, teal, azure, lilac, and violet. Twenty years ago, when I lived in Arizona, I saw mountains glow violet in the light of dawn, fade to pink as the sun rose in the sky, and then turn to blue at dusk. Riding on horseback in the desert, I was mesmerized with the sight of ordinary rocks burning gold, then crimson, all in the space of a moment as the setting sun slanted light to the ground in a constantly shifting angle.

Nothing is actually one color or another—it is only light that makes it so. Of the several hundred colors our eyes can distinguish, each might be brilliant or dull, pale or bold, opaque or translucent, solid or mottled, variegated, even iridescent. With the many words we have to name color, it can still be nearly impossible to describe a specific tint in words alone. Color is in the eyes of the beholder. I've found talking to printers or seamstresses over the phone is useless without sending samples of the color I'm after, and even then, two people might experience a color and see it in very different ways. "Mauve," to some, may be a muddy rose. To others, it is simply pink. "Lemon yellow" is to me a bright, clear shade, warm as the Mediterranean sun. To someone else, it might be sour and flat.

Ancient languages do not abound with words for color. I have read that primitive people began naming colors with black and white only, and then, a while later, added red, leading some scholars to conclude that a sense for color evolved over time. I find this difficult to swallow. Primitive humans depended much more on the natural world than we do, and they must have been even more attuned to light, shadow, and shades of color in their surroundings. But language also evolves with practical experience. Medieval Anglo-Saxons had no word for "orange" because they did not know the fruit in their northern clime. The closest we can find in their language is "jonquil," a flower they knew well, the one we now call "daffodil." It is not really the same color as an orange at all.

The symbolism of colors has also evolved over time. In native cultures, the vibrant, warm colors of red, orange, and yellow are sacred, symbolizing life. Finding the red of their own blood in the pigment of ochre, the earliest humans used red to anoint the bodies of their dead kin. Today, we venerate the purity of white limestone and marble in classical architecture. Yet cleaning of the ancient temples and statuary and the old cathedrals has produced evidence that the stones were often covered with paint in garish red, yellow, and blue, even gilded with gold leaf to make them glitter, celebrating the divine gifts of color and light.

A few churches still celebrate color. At the mission church of San Xavier del Bac outside Tucson, Arizona, I have seen the plaster saints with their lips painted red and their necks hung with bright garlands of orange and pink paper flowers. Designs painted in green, red, and yellow splash pilasters and posts. A statue of the Virgin wears a blue robe, and a silvery crown anchors the lace mantilla on her head. A reclining statue of San Xavier is covered with a yellow blanket. Some people, used to the bloodless white stone and pale marble of modern churches, find this carnival of color a sacrilege. But to the sensibilities of the Mexican American and Papago Indian people who come here, brilliant color is a form of worship.

In Western culture, the virginal, the perfect, and the holy are symbolized by white. Angels are clothed in white, and white is worn by nurses, doctors, and brides. Christ appears to his apostles in shining white robes when transfigured, triumphant over death, divine. White is so closely associated with death that in some cultures it represents mourning. In Asia, "an occurrence of white" is a death or other sad event, and mourners at a funeral wear white.

On a Sunday morning in May, the service at my church is longer than usual to celebrate first communion for a group of first grade children. The little boys wear white shirts with their dark, pressed pants, and their hair is slicked back unnaturally. The little girls are a vision in white, wearing frilly dresses, with white socks, white shoes, and short, stiff white veils. They are like miniature brides. Some carry tiny white purses, white prayer books, or white rosary beads. How well I remember this procession of white at my own first communion and the power of white as a symbol of purification before an important ritual.

We think of white as innocent, a blank page, empty and guileless. Yet when it comes time to match paint to the white walls of my living room, I have found it to be quite complicated. Some white actually has rose in it, some has yellow, and some has gray, making it look warm or cool by degrees. At the paint store, I collect cardboard strips painted and labeled with the imaginative names of these tints: Zurich White, Dover White, Kestrel White, Medici Ivory, Ivory Tusk, White Wool, White Organdy, Paper White, Vellum, Water Chestnut. Just looking through the paint samples and letting my mind wander provokes an afternoon's worth of dreaming. "Off White" looks like an old cotton shirt in need of bleaching. It reminds me of mornings spent bleaching white clothing and hanging it to dry in the sun, watching the fresh, white bloom on the soft fabric of blouses, slips, shorts, and socks. I can almost smell the sharp, clean scent of the bleach.

Like the bees and the birds, we are drawn to color, hunger for it, and whether we are always aware of it or not, are strongly affected by it. Many studies have been conducted on the psychological effects of color. The so-called warm colors with the shorter wavelengths of red, orange, and yellow are stimulants. A red light can increase muscle tension. Yellow paint on the walls of a restaurant can increase hunger. It is said that red flowers and linens on the dinner table will encourage conversation. Because it is so excitable, red has come to mean alert, danger, courage, and power.

The Chinese consider red lucky. At the New Year, children are given gifts of "red money," coins wrapped in bright red paper. The traditional dress of Chinese brides is red. The door of a Chinese home or business may be painted red to attract the flow of *ch'i*, the cosmic energy. Chinese cooks insist on a balance of precious "jade, coral, and ivory" in their recipes, using a combination of green, red, and white ingredients to attract the eye. I have tested the theory, using bright red pepper and green snow peas with white scallops and pasta. My family finds the colorful dish enticing, whereas my serving the dish of plain white pasta and pale scallops hardly merits a yawn.

In a very real sense, the green of growing things and the red of our blood are the two colors we live by. At my annual checkup, the doctor pinches my fingers, looks at the skin under my fingernails, and proclaims me free of the anemia that plagues me. "I don't need a blood test," he says. "I can tell by the color of your skin."

Red blood cells tumbling through the veins under my skin were distributing their load of oxygen, giving my skin its healthy glow. Billions of hemoglobin molecules in these red blood cells carry oxygen, racing back and forth from my lungs to the smallest blood vessels in my fingertips, my eyes, my cheeks. Without the iron in these cells, I would not only be pale, I would be oxygen-starved.

Just to be sure, the nurse pricks my finger and looks at a drop of blood under her microscope, counting the red blood cells in a frame to see if I have a sufficient number. I have thirteen, within the normal limit, but not a high number. She takes more blood and sends it to a laboratory. The detailed report that comes back a few weeks later explains that my red blood cells tend to be larger than normal so that fewer of them will fit in the microscope's frame. I think of these oversize cells waddling through my veins with a certain pleasure, an odd pride in my fat red blood.

The ancients believed heredity was carried in the blood, and we still refer to our ancestors as "blood kin," but in fact red blood cells are packed so full of iron and protein that the nucleus itself has been eliminated, and they cannot reproduce. Fresh red blood cells must be manufactured in the bone marrow to replace those that regularly wear out doing their work.

Just as the hemoglobin that makes our blood red is essential to our health, the chlorophyll that makes plants green provides life to the entire planet. The chlorophyll molecule has been compared to hemoglobin because it has the same donut-ring shape. In chlorophyll, an outer ring of nitrogen surrounds an atom of magnesium. Chlorophyll in plants takes carbon from the air, absorbs the energy of sunlight, and along with water converts carbon dioxide into green leaf, stem, and branch, producing carbohydrates that animals and humans consume and change back to energy again. It is no wonder that the green pigment of chlorophyll produces a color that many believe promotes healing, for without it we could not live.

Orange carotene, thought to have healing properties as well, is also present in the green plant factory, assisting in the process of photosynthesis by trapping the sunlight to be converted into food. In autumn, when photosynthesis stops and the green chlorophyll is no longer needed, it is the range of red, orange, and yellow carotene we see revealed in the "turning" leaves.

In autumn, the front yards of homes in our town are piled up with gold leaves fallen from the towering old maples that line the streets. The forested hills all around us look like artists' palettes dabbed with carmine, cadmium, cinnabar, and sienna.

This is the time of year when my father would disappear for hours on a Saturday afternoon to drive alone into the western Pennsylvania hills, a pilgrim in search of autumn's extravagant colors. In his forty-five years employed by the General Electric Company, he was a man more familiar with factories and steel mills than with forests. Yet he followed autumn's call to the hills flushed with red and gold, an annual ritual meant, I'm sure, to feed his eyes and his spirit.

Now I have acquired the habit of driving down country roads in autumn to be dazzled by hillsides glowing with the jeweled crowns of maple, ash, beech, and oak. I head for the hills as he did, randomly following roads that lead nowhere, losing my way and finding moments of unexpected grace. I see sudden vistas of hillsides in scarlet and gold against a bright cobalt sky, cathedrals of color that move me to prayer.

At the farmer's markets, the wooden stalls are another celebration of color, bright with their displays of organically grown vegetables and fruits: garnet raspberries, ruby tomatoes, dark amethyst eggplants, and emerald-green squash. I buy three ears of jewel-toned corn, the most beautiful I've ever seen. The long, shapely cobs glisten with plump kernels of garnet and amethyst. One of the ears is maroon, so dark it is almost black. Another is a crazy-quilt sampler of varicolored kernels, more colors than I would have imagined possible: kernels of ivory, yellow, lavender, indigo, slate, turquoise, and jade-green. A few are mottled blue and white, speckled as stones. I think of the teachings of the Hopi Corn Clan, who prophesied the coming of the black, yellow, and white races to their land. The Corn Clan was instructed to plant all four colors of corn—red for themselves, black, yellow, and white for the other races. The different colors of corn growing together were intended to remind the people that all races should live in harmony.

But nature does not choose color as we do, for symbol, art, or style. Color in the natural world is more often a function of survival. Pigmentation has purpose: it shields, attracts, warns, and lures. Nasturtiums are no doubt full of the red and orange carotene pigment because it attracts birds to the flower for pollination. Come fall, our yard is full of red holly berries, rose hips, viburnum berries, yew berries, and crab apples, all of which birds will strip from bushes and trees in winter and early spring. I like having these bright dots of red in the winter landscape for their rare color, and I like knowing they provide food for the hungry birds. Birds cannot see the blue shades as well as the red, so those plants like the holly which produce red berries are most apt to attract them.

Unlike the birds, bees and butterflies cannot see red. They do see the ultraviolet waves reflected on flower petals like landing strips lit to attract them and guide them in to the flower's elixir of nectar. In summer, the bees must live in a hallucinogenic, Peter Max world of colors we can only imagine. At both ends of the spectrum, in the ultraviolet and the infrared frequencies, are many shades human eyes do not detect. Within the spectrum of visible light are also many that simply go unnoticed.

Come winter, I stalk the landscape for these more subtle shades. The snowy field of a farm outside of town is etched with the fawn and buff of dried grasses, weeds, and wildflowers. On a hilltop, an oak tree holds on to a few of its russet leaves all winter. Wading through the snow around our cabin, I find goldenrod standing brown and frozen, some stalks with bulbous galls here and there on the stems, spherical cocoons inhabited by the larvae of wasps and flies. The galls are a dusky, burnished gold, as if an artist had gilded them. Wild raspberry vine is a shiny, purplish red, the long, curved whips of its cane covered with buds that will release fringes of green again in a few months. Spidery yellow blossoms still cling to the gray branch of a witch hazel that doesn't bloom until November.

In winter, it is more obvious that each of the spruce, pine, and fir in our yard is a different shade of green. Some are more yellow, some almost entirely blue. The top growth of the blue spruce in our backyard is brown with what seem like hundreds of the pendulous female cones hanging ripe from the new branches that grew in summer. Their seeds will scatter, driven by the wind, transported by birds, planted by squirrels.

In January, driving to work, I chance upon the bold, deep red of sumac fruit by the side of the road. In January, the ivy growing up my back fence is green-mottled reddish gold. I have seen winter ivy exactly this shade in a Japanese watercolor over two hundred years old at the Metropolitan Museum in New York. Centuries ago and a world away, the painter's eye saw the same shades. And on some January mornings, the snow in my backyard is streaked with blue shadows in the sunlight.

Blue, the color of a sunlit sky, has long been considered the most precious color of all. To the ancients it was the color of the vault of heaven, the home of the gods. Blue was once the rarest of natural dyes, and this, along with its celestial origins, made it lucky. Blue is the coveted color of precious lapis lazuli, cobalt, sapphires, and turquoise. Blue is also the color of peace, spirit, truth, and loyalty. Blue calms the nervous system and is thought to induce creativity. Brides still carry "something blue" to their weddings for luck. Bluebirds symbolize happiness. "Blue chips" are the most valuable chips in a poker game, and the so-called blue-chip stocks are the costliest on the market. The highest prize in a competition is often the "blue ribbon." The ruling classes are referred to as "blue bloods."

Blue is the color everyone likes, the one that looks good on anyone, the one interior decorators say is most likely to please their clients. The cypress siding of our house is stained a softly weathered bluish gray. Inside, our kitchen is painted blue and white like Delft china.

On September 30 this year there is a blue moon, one full twice in the same month, a rare and lucky event. It is also the harvest moon, the one closest to the autumn equinox, which has just passed, the moon that once gave light to farmers bringing in their crops, allowing them to work all night. The blue moon rises in the southeast, and it is indeed blue with the cool blue flame of an electric arc, lighting the sky nearly blue again, as if it were day. The dome of heaven is streaked with a few clouds and sparkling with stars. I stand outside in the courtyard, looking up and shivering, for the night is cold.

The moonlight shines on the made and the man-made, on the hedge of yew and on the slate stones of the walk and on the flat blue board of the fence in our courtyard. It shines on the blue juniper and the blue holly and the black cast-iron shade of the lamp on its post at the end of the walk. It makes strange new patterns on familiar objects, cutting blue shadows in shapes shattered by moonlight. How terribly long, I think, would be a month of nights without moonlight, how empty, how afraid we would be without the sun at morning to light the world, and at night, its correspondence, reflected to us from another world.

All night as I try to sleep the moon glides over the blue dome of the sky, and I dream of blue fields where ghostly hands move slowly, like somnambulists, scythes of blue steel in their hands. They slice the hay, and it falls in limp sheaves to the ground.

By morning, the blue moon is gone. As I drive to work, I see fat, round bales of hay lying voluptuously in the fields. And in the shadows made by farmhouses and barns, the grass is thick with blue frost.

The Unequal Hours

And I want, in the hushed moments
when the nameless draws near,
to be among the wise ones—or alone.
RAINER MARIA RILKE, "The Book of Hours"

I sleep less as I grow older, waking often in the hours before dawn. Like the very old, I don't want to miss anything. Waiting for first light, I lie in my bed and pray for the souls of the dead, ask for strength this day when I must teach and write and cook dinner, and keep patience. I repeat the prayers I learned in childhood, until they are as inevitable and steady a beat as the surging of my blood, the ticking of the clock that is my heart.

I rise, dress, make coffee, preparing myself for the day's moments. Looking out at the darkness, I imagine another life, when, cloistered, I might have knelt for hours of contemplation before dawn, broken my fast with bread cooked by the sisters, and then gone to work in the physick garden of herbs. The day would be measured with calls to prayer: matins, lauds, prime, terce, vespers, compline. All one had to do was listen for the bells, and prayers were the drums that beat the rhythm of the hours.

Our word "hour" comes from the Greek *horae*, goddesses of great beauty who presided over the cycles of time: the hours, the seasons, the years. They guarded the gates of heaven, and in spring, they allowed rain to shower the earth and make flowers grow. In Genesis, it is the God of Moses who decrees on the third day of creation: "Let there be lights in the firmament of the heaven to divide the day from the night; and let them be for signs, and for seasons, and for days, and years." In these tales, the secret of time is hidden: the only reliable timepiece is the earth, turning, traveling, season to season, day to day, hour to hour, moment to moment.

We have long paid homage to the hours with song. Native American people rise to salute the sun and sing to the winds of the east, west, north, and south. In ancient India, the ragas of sacred Hindu music were hymns to morning, afternoon, and night. Early Christians gave songs of praise at the first, third, and sixth hours as had the Hebrews for centuries.

Monastic orders in the Middle Ages later formalized the Canonical Hours and read the prayers that came to be known as the Divine Office at regular intervals, making the entire day holy with prayer. The office included prayers to the Holy Virgin, the penitential psalms, a litany to the saints, and, strangely to modern mentality, the Office of the Dead, recited, perhaps, as a reminder of mortality or as a protection against the sudden and unexpected death so common to medieval man. The Book of Hours, a breviary of the office that was often illuminated with miniature paintings in gorgeous color, was the best-seller of its day. *Domine labia mea aperies*, the prayers begin—"Lord, open my lips"—*Et os meum annunciabit laudem tuam*—"And let me sing your praises."

Today it is mainly for their fabulous miniatures that surviving Books of Hours are known. The books are named after their owners, who commissioned them from the leading artists of the day. The "Tres Riches Heures" of the Duc de Berry of France, the most famous example, was illuminated by three different artists and never finished until years after the duke's death. He commissioned at least twenty such books, often appearing himself in the illuminations wearing his favorite color of cerulean blue, one of the most expensive colors to produce. A collector of fine art, books, religious relics, rare plants, and exotic animals, the duke bankrupted himself with his acquisitions so that by the time of his death his estate could not even pay for his funeral. His hours were indeed rich.

The Divine Office may still be heard at certain monasteries that keep up the tradition, where monks know the time for prayers by modern watches and clocks. But in the time before the invention of clocks, or even the shifting sands of the hourglass, there was only sunlight and shadow to reckon the hours of prayer. "Day" meant the sun was shining, and the day was divided into twelve hours, as it had been since ancient times, with the length of shadows marking the time it took the sun to cross the sky. Shadow markers were placed on the walls of churches to indicate the hours for prayers, and later, sundials of bronze set on stone pedestals in the center of the garden, with their pointed gnomons, after the Greek for "interpreter," slanting up to cast a shadow for the hour on the marked face of the dial.

There was more sun in summer than in winter, so the hours of summer were longer and those of winter shorter. As a result, winter and summer hours were called "the unequal hours."

In Saxon England, the hours were called "tides"—eventide, noontide, Yuletide—as if time were pulled across the earth like water. Here, King Alfred the Great wanted a more regulated day. He ordered made a candle with markings at intervals for twelve equal hours. After much experimentation, a tallow was found that would burn down to each marking at twelve regular intervals, and the king's tides were equally divided. The candle clock would take the place of the fickle sun.

At first Alfred was pleased with his invention. With his candle, he could divide the day into equal hours for prayer, study, judgment, counsel, strategy, and war. It is said he took these candles with him everywhere—to the battlefield, too, no doubt, for his rule was seldom peaceful. Like a modern man, he was obsessed with controlling the hours, shaping them to his purpose. He lived only fifty years, but in that time he drove the Danes from his kingdom and learned Latin, translated Saint Augustine's soliloquies and the Christian Psalms, built forts, schools, and churches, and wrote a code of law. Alfred's hours were indeed busy.

But he hadn't accounted for drafts, which could make his candle burn faster and unevenly. It had to be shielded with a cage topped by a shade that was lowered gradually as the day's tides swept on toward darkness. Alfred must have spent his hours craving order—an orderly day, an orderly rule, an orderly England.

In reality, all the hours are unequal. The earth's elliptical orbit around the sun causes it to spin faster at some times than at others. The twenty-four hours we now count each day are merely average divisions of the time it takes the earth to complete one orbit around its own axis; the time varies as much as six minutes from one day to the next. Fixed shadow markers and sundials can't keep up with the uneven earth. Eventually, they become inaccurate. But the fascination with sundials continues if only as symbols of the marking of time.

Sculptor Paul Manship made the world's largest sundial for the 1939 World's Fair in New York. Cast in bronze, the three fates—Past, Present, and Future—stand under the Tree of Life, which holds up a gnomon over eighty feet long. Lachesis, the Present, measures the thread of life passing through her hands, hoping for luck, while Clothos, the Future, spins the thread, leaning forward with her distaff like the figurehead on the prow of a ship sailing into space, and Atropos, the Past, crouches behind them and cuts the thread. The branch of the tree over her head is bare. Perched there is a raven gloating at the outcome of Fate, for each man or woman's thread is of a finite length.

Today, radioactive clocks mark minutes and seconds with great accuracy. These clocks emit electrons to count the seconds at regular, equal intervals, added to or subtracted from to account for the earth's uneven rotation.

Still, the ancient traditions abide, and we reckon the hours by twelve and twelve, the mystic duo decade of cosmic order, a multiplication of the mystical numbers three and four. There are twelve months of the year, twelve knights of the round table, twelve apostles, and twelve Titans, twelve tribes of Israel and twelve gates to the Holy City. There are twelve signs of the zodiac and twelve days of Christmas. Black Elk's vision lasted for twelve days. The Egyptians spoke of the twelve gates of hell where Ra spent the night.

Light comes to me unnoticed at first, sneaking up in a green mist while I am busy dressing or drinking coffee. Then I can see the tall old hemlocks and maples that surround our house, and I know it is day. Outside in the yard I look for flowers to pick for our table, but the petals of the lilies and daisies are still folded like praying hands, and I don't want to disturb them. Perhaps they will pray for me.

I turn pots of yellow marigolds set on the sunny porch so that they will grow straight, and for a while they look as if their backs are turned, but I know that by tomorrow they will have turned around again, looking to the sun. Do we all grow toward the sun, heed its call, listen to its pulsing clock of photons? Deep in the brain, in the hypothalamus, a hormonal clock is triggered by light to make us wake and sleep, dance, sing, and dream, folding and unfolding like the leaves of plants that will follow these circadian—meaning "like a day"—rhythms for weeks even if they are placed in complete darkness.

I watch the light, and in summer at least I can tell the hour with nothing else. I lean toward it as it crosses the sky. I know where to find it, I know its color. At nine in the morning it is white, at three in the afternoon it is briefly, gloriously gold, and by six it is the blue hour, and shadows creep across the lawn.

In August, the light is lower. Our house faces east, and in the morning our roof blocks most of the sunlight from the backyard. The herbs that I grow in pots are already in shadow by two o'clock in the afternoon. The basil and thyme and sage stop growing. The plants stand still, like someone holding her breath, trying to stop the violence of time with silence and stasis, to stop the scissors cutting the thread of life.

The thought of long winter nights frightens me now as it must have frightened the ancients. The sun was going away and might never return. I know why they lit bonfires and beat drums to call it back during the twelve days of chaos that marked the winter solstice. My brain does not make enough of the hormone that keeps my body's time for the unequal hours. From the time of the summer solstice until the autumn equinox I can feel the sun going away, and by October my sleep is disturbed by dreams of a great wind tearing down the house around me. My hair stops growing. I don't sleep for two or three nights in a row; then I sleep for twelve hours during the day. At these times, I must study the sky outside my window to be sure if it is day or night.

The nights grow longer, until there are more hours of darkness than of light. By November, I may sit for hours at my desk with my head down on my arms as if grieving or lie in front of the fire, staring at the flames. I am prone to illness, accidents, and evil dreams.

Modern researchers have given the malady a name: Seasonal Affective Disorder, SAD for short. The very idea of a disease named SAD actually cheers me up, it is so touching. The idea that millions suffer from it and probably always have partially explains the bonfires, the sacrifices and chaos, the fearful dream time, and the senseless revelry of the winter solstice. This is the time of year the Iroquois held their Festival of Dreams, a time out of time when ordinary rules of behavior were abandoned, an otherworldly time when spirits walked from hut to hut. If not welcomed and treated with respect, the spirits were prone to acts of violence. The ancient Celts began their calendar on November first, the feast of Samhain, god of the dead. It was one of their "cross quarter" days, midway between the solstice and the equinox. On the eve of Samhain, time belonged to neither the old year nor the new, the barriers between the two worlds of the living and the dead dissolved. The god of the dead called to his subjects and set them free to roam the earth. Evil spirits were appeased with gifts of the harvest—apples and gourds—or frightened away with bonfires and loud music and dancing. The Christian church, attempting to turn pagan rituals into holy rites, created All Soul's Day to mark the time instead. But All Hallow's Eve still marks a time of seeing into the world of the dead.

I anxiously await the winter solstice, for I know that when the hours of daylight begin to grow, one moment at a time as the earth draws near the sun, my mood will change. To the ancients, the return of the sun meant the return of life itself. And the frenzy of celebration in the last week of December which we now call Christmas is really a substitute for the pagan Saturnalia, when the Roman god Saturn, an ancient agricultural deity, was honored with unrestrained feasting. The Saturnalia lasted for seven days, embracing the winter solstice, from the seventeenth to the twenty-third of December. Courts were closed, schools shut down, and commerce was suspended. Masters served their slaves. All attempts at order were abandoned as the earth veered in its orbit toward the sun. Music, feasting, dancing, and debauchery urged it on its journey.

The feast of Christmas does not appear as December 25 on the calendar until A.D. 336. The fathers of the church chose the time of the Saturnalia, hoping to replace it with a more sedate Christian holy day. But the excesses of Saturn's reign inevitably return at this time of year—you just can't keep a good god down. And many of our Christmas customs are held over from the Saturnalia. The ancient Romans gave each other gifts of dolls at this time, thought to represent even more ancient human sacrifice. They illuminated the darkness with candlelight and bonfires to encourage the sun's return. Wreaths symbolized the cycle of life and death, frankincense was burned for purification.

Watching the world sleep and wake, sleep and wake throughout the changing year must have given us our belief in metamorphosis. At the end of the year, the old man of time, gaunt and bent, relinquishes his scythe to the pink-cheeked cherub of the New Year, and we begin again, innocent, virtuous with resolutions, sated with food and drink, hopeful with the knowledge that although we age along with the year, the babe will always come again, and out of the darkness comes light.

Resting after a long season of growth, our woods at the end of August are still, and the drone of locusts makes a lazy, throbbing pulse that sounds like "living, living, living . . ." Walking down the lane to our cabin, I smell the perfume of the last wild raspberries and find them bunched on the vines like bloody little fists. Spiders have thrown their webs on the grass, sparkling nets of fine silver that remind me of frost, and as I wander through the raspberry patch I hear a regular, heavy thud in the distance, echoing across the hills like gunshots. I stand still and listen a few moments before I can determine it is only a neighbor setting fence posts to keep in his sheep on the hill.

In the highlands, summer is short. Purple asters already dot the fields, and everywhere is the smell of autumn coming, a smell made of rotting leaves, smoke, pine tar, and dust. I carry a canvas bag and a pair of scissors for cutting the last of the wild mint before frost can take it. I know where it grows, down in the rocky streambed, and I push my way toward it through brittle blackberry vine, plush piles of maple leaves, and pine cones sticky and white with tar at my feet. As I come into view of our pond, ten young ducks and their parents rise up from the water squawking, swooping off in an indignant line of twelve. These wild things, though they may nest here for years to come, will never waste their time in knowing me. Soon, the unequal hours will trigger their flight south, for the diminishing day tells them it is time to go. Navigating by sunlight and the magnetic field of the earth turning in space, they will leave and then return to the same nesting places year after year, the parents showing the younger ones the way before they die.

I am leaving, too, and as I walk back to the road I startle three young deer by the edge of the wood. They turn their amber heads to stare, their big ears pointed up and twitching, their long, slim legs and velvety flanks taut and still. They have an eagerness about them, already poised to leap at the sound of a rifle shot.

The Way of the Garden

Gardening is an exploration of a place close to home.
MICHAEL POLLAN,
Second Nature: A Gardener's Education

On the eighth day of March, there are two feet of freshly fallen snow piled up around our house. Standing on the bank in our backyard is the bronze figure of a nude woman, a garden nymph Bill sculpted many years ago. Buried up to her armpits in snow, she holds out her hands palms up in a gesture of supplication. I turn up the heat indoors and wonder if winter will ever end. It is time to start thinking about our garden.

I shop for seed trays and add a packet of sweet basil to the others waiting in a round tin: early harvest tomatoes, miniature yellow marigolds, white zinnias, blue and red salvia, nasturtium, sunflowers, moonflowers, and morning glories. I open the box that came in the mail last week and unpack bags of seed-starting formula. I clear the table in our bedroom where the seedlings will grow under a fluorescent light meant to imitate the sun.

These are all acts of hope.

On March 21, just after the spring equinox and two days from the new moon, I plant the first seeds for our kitchen garden: tomatoes and sweet basil, both seeds that germinate easily and grow quickly for me indoors. This is a yearly ritual of almost religious significance. The packets of seeds must be set out, seed trays filled with soil and soaked in water. I part small furrows in the soil to receive each seed and carefully tear open the paper envelopes. The tomato seeds are flat and pink, the sweet basil seeds mere black grains. Like all rituals, this is a ceremony of transformation, for these dry specks of life will soon make a miracle. I drop seeds into the furrows, covering each one with a bit of soil, and water them.

I don't have a greenhouse for my seedlings, just a few square feet in my sewing room where there is an old cedar chest next to a floorboard heater. Propped over the heat on the edge of the cedar chest, with moisture trapped by a transparent plastic roof, the seeds sprout eagerly in just three days. There is still snow on the ground from last week's storm, but already I can move this batch of seedlings from the sewing room and watch them produce green stem and leaf, the slim threads of their roots stitching into the growing medium in the seed pots. As they grow, the long, slim leaves of a few of the tomato seedlings cling to the husk of the seed that germinated them. Carefully, I pick off the husk. A pair of pointed leaves springs out like a dancer's legs, free to spread under the light in an upside-down arabesque.

Watching the seedlings grow cheers me as a cold, wet March drags on. The plants grow quickly, and I transfer them from trays to peat pots and empty milk cartons we've been saving. The tomato plants will send out roots from their stems, so we bury the stems in a mixture of soil and starting formula in the milk cartons and let the plants develop more roots. When the weather starts to warm up in May the plants will be big enough to move over to Bill's studio downtown, where there is more room and a large bank of south-facing windows. There the seedlings will get sun for a while until our traditional planting time of Memorial Day weekend. In the meantime, some of the people going in and out of the post office across the street will look up at the windows filled with green leaf and stem, growing toward the light. Those who are gardeners know what's happening and comment on the progress of the plants.

April nearly destroys hope, bringing still more snow and a storm so unexpectedly severe that Bill puts his truck in the ditch one morning at the top of an icy hill. He is unhurt, but the truck is mangled. Not until the first week of May with its evening rains, full moon, and warm, bright days does the garden respond with vigor. This is the year our weeping crab apple and our azalea blossom, clumps of trillium, grape hyacinths, narcissus, yellow cowslips and pink primroses fill the bank in front of our house, and violets spread out over the lawn.

Bending to pick handfuls of the tiny, purplish-blue flowers on a cool, sunny morning, I remember what a fortune teller said to me once long ago. Gazing at my palm, she said simply, "I see you surrounded by violets." And so I am. Fulfilling this strange destiny, I walk through the garden in a vaguely understood state of grace. Did she see me in this moment at a turning point, a place where life takes me in some new direction or at a place I have come to in peace after many trials? Or was it the happiness of my marriage, the purchase of this home Bill and I own, the tending of the garden which brings me joy? Why did she see me illuminated here in her second sight, surrounded by violets?

This year the violets have spread their taproots enthusiastically across the lawn. I suspect they thrived over the long winter with its constant snow cover. The snow is actually good for plants waiting beneath the soil. Like a layer of mulch, snow insulates the ground and keeps it moist. I remember the gardeners in my family commenting during a snowy winter, "good snow, good garden." I pick the purple violets blooming all over our back lawn and the hybrids they have produced, mostly white, with only the very center blushing purple. Then I search the house for tiny vases to hold them.

I look for the pure white violets that grow on our bank, but they're not out yet. I have to wait a week, and then everything white comes out at once: white violets, white dogwood, and white lilac with its intoxicating perfume. Clothed in white for a few brief days, the garden looks like a home for angels.

In cultures worldwide, the garden represents an earthly paradise, a place touched by God. The word "paradise" actually comes from the ancient Persian word for "walled garden." In the walled gardens of medieval monasteries, European monks made "paradise gardens" of flowers and herbs where they could contemplate God's divine nature in his creations. In the medieval monasteries of Europe, the rule of St. Benedict specified three different kinds of gardens to keep the monks self-sufficient and protected from the outside world. The paradise garden gave them pleasure and showed them the glory of God. The kitchen garden provided them with food. And the physick garden contained medicinal herbs, sometimes hundreds of them, to treat everything from head lice to snakebites.

Zen Buddhist monks make gardens of sand, gravel, and

a few thoughtfully placed rocks. These "dry gardens" are themselves a manifestation of Zen thought, "gardens of the mind." The ancient gardens of Japanese emperors were more elaborate paradise gardens called "pure land," designed in the form of mandalas and meant as homes for Amida, the Buddha of Infinite Light. Those who worshiped him devoutly, it was thought, would at death be reborn not to another lifetime on earth but to an immortal existence in the gardens of paradise.

The Chinese thought gardens could help one to achieve immortality, or at least venerable old age, which was the next best thing. The serenity of a beautiful garden was thought to promote long life by removing one from stress and strain. One could meditate on long life by surrounding one's garden with symbols of happiness and longevity found in nature, like the peony, which also symbolized wealth in its many petals; the chrysanthemum, which lasted longer than any other flower; the pine tree, which remained ever green; and the magic peach, food of the immortals. One could also keep long-lived animals like the tortoise or the crane in such a garden for inspiration.

Gardens have made spiritual metaphor for millennia. One of the Buddhist sutras tells of an unskilled farmer who threw away his rubbish and bought manure from other farmers to put on his garden. The skilled farmer, however, collected his own stinking garbage as compost and used it to fertilize his crops. Thus the sutra teaches that those unskilled at spiritual development will try to reject their own faults— their garbage—and attempt to buy spiritual enlightenment from others or emulate another who seems to be without faults. But the wise man acknowledges his own faults and tills them into his soil. By accepting our faults and working with them, we grow and perfect ourselves.

Jesus of Nazareth spoke often of gardens. He told of the sower, who saw some seeds fall by the wayside, where fowl came and devoured them, and some seeds fall upon stony places, where they sprang up but were soon scorched by the sun and withered away. Some seeds fell among thorns, and the thorns rose up and choked them. But some fell onto good ground and brought forth fruit. And when Jesus confronted his own moment of truth, he withdrew into the garden at Gethsemane.

No one should be without a garden, even if it is indoors or on a city rooftop. We simply weren't meant to live without green, growing things around us. Seeing something grow is psychologically uplifting, and many ordinary houseplants have practical benefits. Plants like the Boston fern, the philodendron, and the weeping fig will remove formaldehyde and carbon dioxide from the air in a home or office.

In my family, gardening is an old tradition unchanged by modern convenience. My grandfather Salvatore and his ancestors farmed the stony terraces of Italy, and when he came to America, he made gardens for a living. He was a man always happy out-of-doors, and I never knew him to want anything more. His first home in America was on a city street in Pittsburgh, with a tiny yard, but my mother remembers the fig tree he lovingly tended in a container, to remind him of the Mediterranean climate. The family pooled their resources early on to purchase a plot of suburban farmland where they grew vegetables. Later, in his retirement years, he built a large stone house with several acres of gardens where my brother and I spent weekends wandering. The hillside was planted with pear trees that bore fragrant fruit. Up and down the long stone retaining wall that edged his driveway were rows of pink, red, and white peonies that burst into voluptuous bloom early in summer. Outside the kitchen door was the small, sunny cook's garden of herbs, tomatoes, and beans and further up the hill behind the house a larger vegetable garden for growing melons, onions, and peppers.

When Salvatore died, my grandmother Concetta gradually moved into smaller houses but always with a garden of some kind. Her last home was an apartment with a concrete terrace, where on the day she died a pot of basil and a pot of marigolds grew.

My grandfather's last act of garden making was building the many stone walls enclosing the gardens of my mother's home. Several large boulders came out of the ground when the foundation was dug and were rolled down into the backyard while the house was being built. These were split with a jackhammer to make the garden walls. By then nearly seventy, he placed his ubiquitous cigar down on a nearby rock and slowly fit the stones together, tapping them with a small hand mallet to shape them, building up dry walls to retain the soil on a bank or to define the area around a flower bed. Now, twenty-five years later, these walls still stand, rooted in the earth like old dragon bones.

The Japanese consider the placement of rocks as important to a garden as the plants, choosing rocks for their unusual shapes or large size to represent the mountaintop in miniature. A garden can be created even in a shady place, with mosses, a trickle of water, and a few beautiful rocks to give the tiniest corner a cherished air of *wabi*, a melancholy harmony, a longing for the distant wilderness, a wistfulness considered beautiful in the Japanese garden. Many times, on a city street, I have glimpsed these miniature heavens from behind a slatted fence, tucked into a narrow alley or the corner of a handkerchief-sized lawn, with a few plants, perhaps a fern, some moss, and a beautiful rock. Even indoors, such a garden can be created for a tabletop with a tray of well-watered moss, a few unusual rocks, or a miniature bonsai tree.

In the larger Japanese gardens, vistas beyond the garden are as important as the garden itself. Stepping-stones are carefully placed so as to guide one's appreciation of this "borrowed" scenery, called *shakkei*. Passing slowly from one stone to another, the viewer stops to contemplate harmony and form in a vista from first one angle and then another, very much as one would walk from one landscape painting to another in an art gallery. Teiji Itoh, author of many books about Japanese garden aesthetics, speaks of the concept of *mitate* encouraged by this form of contemplation, a kind of enlightenment, when "forced to look, led to observe, one suddenly sees, as though with new eyes, a world of beauty in the most ordinary things."

The Japanese garden strives to imitate nature by using stones and plants to form mountains, forests, and even oceans and streams in miniature. The effects on both the mind and the eye are magical. Hedges are trimmed and sculpted to resemble ocean waves. The stark white gravel of the Zen garden is raked in the form of waves to resemble flowing water. The work of cleaning and raking the gravel is a spiritual discipline, an exercise in patience and concentration, and if you think it looks easy, try doing it sometime. You may gain more respect for the practice and what it teaches.

The patterns made in the gravel have names: ripples called

sazanami, larger waves called *uneri*, whirlpools called *uzu-maki-mon*, the fish-scale-shaped "blue" waves called *seigaiha*, and the concentric circles raked around rocks called *uzumon*. In one of the most famous of Kyoto's many beautiful gardens, a stone shaped like a boat "rides" a gravel "river" raked in long, flowing lines, symbolizing the journey of the soul through life.

Elaborate ceremony and ritual surround the choice of the all-important rocks and paving stones in a Japanese garden. The stones are selected with a sculptor's eye for their shape, size, and color. One large, one medium, and one smaller stone placed together represent heaven, earth, and man. Stepping-stones are never on a straight line and are placed in configurations suggesting natural patterns. Stones placed in a zigzag pattern are called "flight of geese." Another pattern is called "plover" because it suggests the tracks left in the sand by a plover. Still another made of small stones scattered in groups is called "fallen flowers."

The aesthetic of *sabi* refers to the patina, or surface appearance of the rock and other objects in the garden, showing how they have aged, perhaps acquiring moss, lichens, or streaks of mineral deposits from falling water. The garden should look as if it has been there a long time—this is *sabi*. So important is this effect to a Japanese garden that care must be taken to erase the appearance that the garden has been worked on. There is a story of a Japanese tea master carefully sweeping the fallen leaves from his tea garden and then deliberately shaking a tree so that three perfect leaves fell on the path.

The effect must also be tastefully understated in a way the Japanese call *shibui*. Bill tells me the story of a tea master who cut down all but one perfect chrysanthemum in his garden before his guests arrived for the ceremony. The one perfect flower was better than a whole garden because it focused appreciation on true beauty rather than on ostentatious display. The focus on simplicity, small details, and natural beauty in the garden are all essential to the effect of the tea ceremony itself, which promotes harmony, reverence, purity, and tranquillity in its ritualized actions, performed slowly, with great concentration.

Through *wabi, sabi,* and *shibui,* the Japanese tea garden achieves a unique serenity. It is a place to seek *roji,* a Buddhist concept referring to the mindfulness that can be practiced while performing simple tasks. Stripping away all pretense, drawing significance to each utilitarian object and gesture, one distracts the mind from stress, sorrow, and confusion. In the garden, one finds peace.

After studying the aesthetics of the Japanese garden, I look on our walled courtyard with new eyes. The paving stones placed by the landscaper move not in a straight line to the front door, but in a shallow curve, edged with rhododendrons, mostly the native variety called *Rhododendron maximum.* The non-native hybrids, called *Nova zembla,* are doing poorly, and we had to remove one of them this spring, so damaged was it by the winter storms. But the native rhododendrons are thriving. Large stones of weathered granite with appropriate *sabi* have been placed at the beginning and the end of the path to focus attention. As dictated by Japanese garden manuals, they are not simply set on the ground but half buried in it, which actually makes them appear larger, and older, as if they have always been there.

I work in the courtyard on a warm morning in May, weeding, pruning, trimming, watering plants, and then sweeping the stone pathways and the redwood planks on the deck. Straightening up to rest for a moment after trimming a long, low hedge, I look out on the borrowed view of my neighbor's yard. The plum tree is blooming deep pink, and white apple blossoms drift to the ground. Then I notice that something extraordinary is happening. The white ships of fluff carrying dandelion seeds come floating over the lawn, slowly, at first just a few here and there, and then, a whole fleet of them, in waves by the hundreds, moving up and down in the warm air currents, until it seems a soft snow is falling on the yard.

As randomly as they appear to drift and dodge, these white parachutes are ripe with purpose, transporting their cargo in downy arks that roll across, over, and through the trees. Weightless, they elude my attempts to grab one in my hand until I sit perfectly still for a moment in a chair on the deck and watch the migration more quietly. Only then does one land lightly in my palm. I let it go, and the breeze lifts it swiftly up and out of sight. The dandelion ships catch on tall blades of grass, stick to wet spots on the walk where I have been watering our flower beds, and fall against the screen door leading to the bedroom. When I go inside, they follow me, landing on my desk and my bed. Our ravens perch on the tips of the spruce trees and peer down at the show, announcing their own astonishment in raspy squawks. The dandelion snow continues all morning while I sip tea, listen to the ravens squawking and the other birds singing, and watch the dancing white dandelion seeds as I read from Kenneth Rexroth's *One Hundred Poems from the Chinese* and *One Hundred Poems from the Japanese*:

The flowers whirl away
In the wind like snow.
The thing that falls away
Is myself.

In my narrow room, I throw
Wide the window, and let in
The profound lasciviousness
Of Spring.

The pear blossoms are pure
White against the blue green willows.
The willow cotton blows in the wind.
The city is full of flying pear flowers.
The petals fallen on the balcony look like snow.
How many Spring Festivals are we born to see?

And from Walt Whitman I read:

Thou, soul, unloosend'—the restlessness after I know not what:
Come, let us lag here no longer, let us be up and away!
O if one could but fly like a bird!
O to escape, to sail forth as in a ship!
To glide with thee O soul, o'er all, in all, as a ship o'er the waters;
Gathering these hints, the preludes, the blue sky, the grass, the
    morning drops of dew . . .

Winter is finally past, and the gate to my garden stands
open. Looking through the shadows under our trees, I see
sunlight glowing green on the lawn and the stiff spines of the
holly, dazzling the crimson azaleas and the purple rhododen-

drons. In back of our house, we have turned over the ground to ready it for vegetables and herbs. I watch as my neighbor, an avid gardener who has battled a serious illness throughout the cold and dark of the winter months, walks slowly out on the lawn behind his house to enjoy the sunshine. Many times, we have worked silently together in our gardens, weeding and tilling, watching, watering, and feeding the plants. Today he does not see me, concentrating only on making his legs move. Taking a few halting steps, he stops, lifts his head for a moment, and looks out on the garden with hope.

Water Music

Everything flows.

LAO TZU

It was late in July 1978 that I came home after living for four years in the desert Southwest. Just before sunset, emerging in my car from the darkness of a tunnel carved out of one of Pittsburgh's many hills, I crossed one of its many bridges—and plunged into a state of sensory overload. I was intoxicated by the abundance of water. Everything I saw looked saturated. An incalculable amount of water flowed by in the Allegheny River every moment, water in the sky, in streams and creeks and puddles and ponds. Allegheny River Boulevard was lined with trees so green they were dazzling, every branch and leaf dripping with moisture. This place where the three rivers of the Allegheny, the Monongahela, and the Ohio meet was lush with water in a way I had never appreciated in all the years I had lived there. Why had I never noticed this glorious abundance of water before?

The desert has its own beauty, and in the years I lived in Arizona I learned to love its surreal landscapes and fiery colors. But after four years gazing at the desert's sun-baked glazes of gold, red, and brown, I was mesmerized by the fluid washes of blue, gray, and green of the rivers in my own hometown. Here I could smell water in the air, feel it on my skin, taste it, drink it freely, immerse myself in it in a way that was simply not allowed in Arizona. There, precious groundwater was doled out in rationed portions, the focus of old wars and endless new debates. There, one could not plant a garden, plan an automobile trip, or even do the laundry without first thinking—will there be enough water?

Every year, a few desperate souls perished when their vehicles broke down and they were lost in the desert with no water. I have never forgotten the story published one year in Arizona newspapers of three Nicaraguan refugees stranded without water in the desert south of Tucson. Left there to die after they had paid for safe passage to the United States, one went for help and the other two drank their own urine for three days to survive until they were rescued. I have never forgotten the day I returned to the watery Northeast, dazed by its riches. I have tried not to take water for granted again.

Without thinking of it most of the time, we spend the day drawing water, pouring it, drinking it, washing in it, storing it, emptying it, and drawing it again to keep ourselves alive. How could we toil in the sun without the sweat our bodies release to cool us and the water we drink to replace it? How could we grieve our dead without the healing flow of tears? How could we make a new life without the water carrying seed to the womb? Suspended in an internal sea, the human embryo takes shape floating in the waters of the womb. It comes out in a flood. When my daughter-in-law Palma gave birth to her first child, she had such a strong impression of flowing water that she decided to name her baby Meryn, meaning "of the sea."

Our true element may be water. The human body is nearly three-quarters water. Water plumps the tissues of our skin, our muscles, our brain. We go through several quarts of water each day, using it to metabolize food, send life to every cell, and cool off the heat produced in the process. We can survive for weeks without food, shelter, clothing, or tools, but we cannot live a day without water.

I grew up in sight of rivers, but it was not until I graduated from high school that I first saw the sea—or rather, first smelled it. Driving south from Pittsburgh and headed for the beaches of North Carolina, my friends and I crossed Maryland and reached the shores of Chesapeake Bay. Rolling down the car window, I stuck out my head and for the first time breathed in the scent of ocean water, redolent with salt, shell, and seaweed. When at last we reached the beach in Nags Head, I walked along the sand and felt for the first time the insistent tug of the tides.

Since then I have listened to the music of more than one ocean. On the coast of Maine, I have heard the waters of the Atlantic surge up to rocky shores while I climbed among the rocks to pick the sea lavender that grows there in tidal pools. On the island of St. John in the Caribbean, I slept on an open porch under a tent of mosquito net, surrounded by climbing vines of hibiscus and bougainvillea, waking to the soft strains of waves lapping on the beach. Island dwellers there collected the precious rainwater for their homes in anxiously guarded cisterns. Our friends Rudy and Irene Patton, who owned a jewelry store in the town of Cruz Bay, made necklaces of Spanish silver salvaged from wrecks that lay sleeping on the ocean floor and bracelets out of pieces of sea fan salvaged from the beach and invested with silver.

In Mexico, I saw the ocean trapped in the Gulf of California, lying flat and still. Off the coast of Malibu, in southern California, it was blue and noisy and beaten into Florentine gold in the setting sun. In northern California, I stayed for a few days in a bungalow built on the cliff overlooking Muir Beach in Marin County. Perching on the railing at the very edge of the house's tiny deck, I could see the gray ocean rolling in to crash against tall, black rocks that stood out in the fog like mystic sentinels. Pelicans floated over the beach as I walked along the sand by day. At night, I fell asleep to the murmuring of the waves, whispered like a mantra to my dreaming ear.

San Francisco Bay's waters are gray much of the time, shrouded with wet mists and fog that burns off briefly at midday, only to descend again in the afternoon. Further up the coast, at Cape Mendocino, the sea bears a veneer of dark blue. Thick beds of brown kelp float near the shoreline and wash up on the narrow beaches in tangled ropes. I have walked along the headlands there for hours, listening to the constant music of the waves and watching the patterns of white foam on the rocks. Now and then the speckled head of a seal would bob up in the water. Ocean mists bathe the coastal forests, creating a water-rich environment for the giant redwoods.

If we were a logical race of beings, we would call our planet not "Earth" but rather "Water." Seen from space, it is the blue planet, blue with the water that covers a full three-quarters of its surface, water pulled continuously into motion by the moon, whipped by the wind and warmed by the sun. The water that flows daily through earth and sky—what scientists call the hydrosphere—consists of some 330 million cubic miles of water in constant motion. Moving through the hydrologic cycle of evaporation, transpiration, condensation, and precipitation, water shapes and sustains the life of our planet. Oceans regulate the earth's temperature, absorbing solar energy in summer and releasing it in winter. Water glitters in the polar ice caps and shines in deep volcanic craters. Water fills the long fingers of glacial lakes, foams over cliffs and through canyons, and rushes along in streams. Water forms white clouds and falls in gray sheets of rain, filling river basins and hanging over coastlines in banks of mist and fog. Water is magically transformed from liquid to gas, from gas to liquid, to solid ice, and then to liquid again. No other element takes so many forms.

The small molecules of water ought to be gaseous. But water molecules—made up of two positively charged atoms of hydrogen and one negatively charged atom of oxygen—form chains like magnets strung together by their opposing charges. They stick to other molecules, and this makes them liquid. Water attracts. Water's surface tension also gives it a glassy mirror top, a film that makes a dance floor for a spider's legs.

Water shapes every inch of the land, washing down sediments from mountaintops, cutting canyons and caves, sawing away at beaches. The sea has been nearly everywhere at one time or another. In the Cretaceous period, 150 million years ago, an inland sea engulfed half of North America. The British Isles were submerged, along with Russia and half of Asia. Marine fossils have been found on the peaks of the Himalayas.

Water creates sculptures in our yard whenever it rains. I have planted nasturtium vines to curl up strings tacked to a post, lifting their saucer-shaped leaves on long, narrow stems, and in a drizzle, raindrops explode as they touch the upturned saucers of these leaves, some of them six inches across. On each leaf I see a white blur, as if tiny insects are hovering, but it is only the rain water dispersing. In the space of a moment it collects again, rolled into a silver bead that settles at the depression in the saucer of each leaf. As the rain falls, the silver beads at the bottom of each saucer roll around, growing fatter, some nearly an inch in diameter, attracting more raindrops. Thick and glassy, they magnify the white veins on the green leaf underneath them and reflect my face leaning over them. When a light breeze stirs the vines, the leaves tip one by one, heavy with water, and the silver beads of water fall, splashing the leaves below them before dropping to the ground. The wet leaves hang with necklaces of silver beads clinging underneath.

On cold days in November, our bare trees are transformed when droplets of water cling to black branches, capturing the scant afternoon light, and they appear to be hung with diamonds.

I used to hate getting caught in the rain. I took umbrellas and raincoats with me at the slightest hint of a storm. I had an extensive collection of boots, jackets, waterproofed raincoats, and plastic hats to protect me from rain. I didn't like getting my clothes wet or my hair damp or my shoes stained with water. Now, I'm likely to go out and stand in the rain without so much as a hat to cover my head, so eager am I for the rainwater to touch me.

I can tell when it's about to rain. All day, I have a headache. Before the storm arrives, I hear a chorus of birds chirping anxiously outside. In their tiny bones, more even than my own, they must feel the change of pressure in the air. Their songs warn each other to take shelter. I can time the arrival of the storm this way—in an hour, the first raindrops will fall, making dark spots on the planks of our deck until the wood is completely wet and shiny, reflecting purple and red flowers in terra-cotta pots and a blue watering can by the rail. All over the floor of the deck, raindrops make concentric circles in the pooling water where they form and dissipate in rippling bull's-eyes. Then I go out and stand in the rain, letting it fall on my hair, on my bare hands, washing my face, wetting my lips, dampening my shirt. Thunder rumbles overhead, a streak of lightning tears through dark clouds, and the charge of electricity in the air is invigorating. I feel elated, and my headache is gone.

Rain heightens the senses. Some people say they can smell the rain coming. Actually, it is everything they are smelling. Even before the rain begins to fall, moisture in the air allows the sense of smell to work better. Rainwater washes surfaces slick and bright with color. As adults trained to be fastidious, we forget how delightful rain makes things to the touch, but if you watch a group of children playing in the rain, you'll remember. Rain makes great puddles to splash in, gorgeous, gooey mud to stamp in, slippery wet grass to slide in. Best of all to me is the sound of rain—the lullaby it sings falling on trees and lawns and its pounding rhythms on the roof.

On a Sunday in August, I feel stiff all day, waiting for rain, knowing from the weather report that it's raining in Chicago and a storm is on its way east. But it's not until the following morning that I'm roused from a heavy sleep by the sound of rain pounding on the roof like a primitive drumming. The sensation of being under a roof while rain beats against it is so pleasant I wonder if it has to do with a racial memory of being sheltered from rain in a Neolithic cave.

By its very presence, water purifies and sanctifies. After rain on a summer day, the paving stones in our courtyard shine with the water feeding the lichens and mosses that grow there. Here and there, small depressions in the stones fill with water, making tiny pools. The grass is bright and soft with rain, spiderwebs sparkle with drops of rain, the broad leaves of the dogwood and the rhododendrons and the beeches glisten with rain. Wet with rainwater, the greens and reds of the garden are deeper, more reflective. If this were a Japanese garden, it would be a fine time for serving tea. The impression of cleansing is a necessary element to the tea ceremony. If it has not rained, the host must wet down the garden path with water before the guests arrive. There is a basin of water at the entrance to the tea garden, where guests wash their hands and rinse their mouths as they do at the entry to a shrine.

In Catholic churches, a font of holy water stands at the entrance to the sanctuary. In my youth, one never entered the church without dipping one's fingers into this water and crossing oneself in a gesture of purification. A sick person could obtain vials of water from faraway springs and wells visited by saints and drink it in hopes of a cure. On feast days, the priest walked among us, sprinkling holy water from a perforated globe fitted on the end of a long staff. As he passed, he shook the staff high in the air over my head, and I felt a few drops of the holy water dampening my cheek.

Places where water flows in rivers or rises unaided to bless the earth in springs are perennial sources of holiness, and pilgrims still seek out sacred wells and springs for healing. Because water is so closely associated with the female, these are places where female goddesses and saints are apt to appear. For six months in 1858, a fourteen-year-old French peasant girl named Bernadette Soubirous saw the Virgin Mary at a grotto on the bank of a stream in Lourdes. In Bernadette's visions, the Holy Mother revealed to her the source of an underground spring. Since then, these waters have been credited with miraculous cures, and even in our age of medical science, Lourdes is visited by three million people a year, fifty thousand of them sick or disabled, seeking a miraculous cure from Our Lady of Lourdes.

The source of all life, water is always associated with the mother. To dive beneath the waters is to return to spirit, baptized, purified, and cleansed of evil. To rise from the waters, like Aphrodite, born of sea foam and carried to land by the breath of Zephyrus, the wind, is to become manifest in the world. To cross the river—the river Jordan, the river Styx, the river of forgetfulness, Lethe—is to leave human form and join the souls in the world beyond death, on the other shore.

The water that falls in raindrops on the roof of my house today is the same water that danced in the sacred springs of Delphi and Chartres, the same water that baptized Bernadette at Lourdes, the same water that filled the basin of the Mediterranean and floated the ships of Ulysses. The water created in the steam of primordial volcanoes eons ago is the same water that sings to the beaches of Cape Cod and Cape Mendocino today. We have no new source for the fountain of all life—we must protect what water exists now.

It was on the Mendocino headlands overlooking the Pacific Ocean that I saw each drop of water in the ocean spray singing with an internal light, a vision of power in the atoms of water blowing in with the wind on the beach.

I was sitting at the edge of a cliff, watching the waves move rhythmically toward the shore, listening to the urgent crescendo of sound enfolding me in its spell as the tide rose, and

I saw for a moment another reality, one that must be there always but goes unnoticed. With the setting sun and the ocean breeze on my face, I saw the spirit of water, and it sang to me of the unending power of life and love. I could not call its name, but I heard its voice.

In ancient times, the spirits of the natural world had names and even personalities. To the Greeks, every stream, spring, and pool was blessed by water nymphs. Nymphs who frequented brooks were called *naiads*. In rivers and streams were *potamids*, and in springs, *crenae*. The water nymphs were thought to live in grottoes near flowing water, and they were always young and beautiful. They cured the sick and gave prophecies. Related to the water nymphs were the *hyades*, seven nymphs who cared for Zeus in his infancy. They were rewarded for their loyalty with a home in the sky and became stars. Their name means "the rainy ones," and their appearance in the heavens in May signaled the beginning of rainy weather.

In arid places, the need for water created fearsome rain gods like the Aztec's Tlaloc. Tlaloc demanded the sacrifice of infants and children, and the dying children's tears were thought to bring the rain.

How people raised crops in the arid deserts of our own Southwest has always seemed a miracle to me, knowing how little rain comes to the mesas. For some time, anthropologists wondered if the climate had been different when the ancient Anasazi farmed there. We now know that the native people of the Southwest practiced precise methods of flood control and irrigation to water their fields. Carefully protected from desiccating wind by hedges of sagebrush and cornstalks, their fields held just enough water from the spring flood to grow crops. Elaborate rituals of prayer, song, and dance accompanied the precise choice of a field for planting and the preparation of the ground. But the people were not only wishing for rain, praying for rain, or dancing for rain. They were investing in it, making the best possible use of the precious water that came perhaps once a year but provided, if carefully channeled, all they needed to grow their sacred corn.

Here in western New York the sound of thundering waters is never far away. The land bears the scars of the Ice Age in gullies, cliffs, gorges, and lakes carved out of the hills by glaciers ten thousand years ago. Water cascades down cliffs and through gorges at Glens Falls and Seneca Falls, Honeoye Falls, Skaneateles Falls, Watkins Glen, and Buttermilk Falls outside Ithaca. The Niagara River spills into Canada with a grandeur that draws tourists from all over the world. A half million tons of water plunge 186 feet through the gorge of shale and limestone at Niagara Falls.

In the heart of downtown Rochester, the Genesee River spills down over a cliff before heading north to Lake Ontario. On the map, the Genesee looks like a ball of string flung open, kinked and curled as it winds through Livingston and Wyoming Counties, twisting and turning, sidestepping hills, stumbling, falling, slipping over cliffs as it goes past the towns of Rush, West Rush, Avon, Geneseo, and Castile. At Letchworth State Park it falls three times through a gorge at the edge of William P. Letchworth's lawn. Letchworth built himself a home there called Glen Iris, now a restaurant and inn. A million tourists come through the park each year, standing at the edge of Letchworth's lawn and walking through the gorge, listening to the music of the thundering falls. On warm summer days, the lawn overlooking the falls is a popular place for weddings.

But if you follow the river from Letchworth and head south

on Route 19A, you cross the invisible line dividing Livingston County from Allegany County, and while the country here is just as beautiful, this is the land that the tourism industry forgot. Here there are no information centers, no tour buses, no signs to proclaim the charms of our county. The pride of those here who don't believe in such things once annoyed me. The people who own businesses will often talk wistfully of the dollars to be made promoting our corner of the state— dollars, I might add, badly needed both for jobs and for the dwindling tax base. But there is also an ambiguity to every discussion I've heard, a self-defeating tone that puzzled me at first. "What we don't want," I remember one business leader saying, emotion breaking in his voice, "are a bunch of tourists hopping off the bus to gawk for an hour, paw over the merchandise, and leave."

At first, I was puzzled. Why not try to profit from the interest city folk have in getting away from the cities? But after living here for some years, I've come to understand, even to sympathize. There is a ghostly beauty here, a fragile fabric of peace, a serenity made of one part stubborn nostalgia for the agrarian past, one part escapism, and another part pure meditative solitude. To turn that into a product to be marketed would be to change it irrevocably, to destroy the very source of its sweetness to the artists and writers like myself who have settled here. To commercialize the beauty we live with here every day might create jobs and improve life in a material way. And then there would surely be no reason for us to live here.

And here too is the music of falling water. Driving north toward Letchworth, I turn off Route 19A between Rossburg and Fillmore and pass through the little town of Wiscoy, where a few dozen houses cluster on either side of the road. Many of them are old farmhouses neatly and lovingly restored by retirees, with lace curtains at the windows and fresh coats of paint on the eaves. Here and there are the old barns, too, for like most of the county, this was once a farming community.

If you follow the road past these houses, you come to a bridge over the river, and there you can stop to see the falls at Wiscoy. There is no parking lot. There's space for four cars by the red brick power plant on the left and a turnoff around the bend past the bridge on the right, with enough space for a few more cars. There are no campgrounds, no restaurants, no inns, no gift shops, no concession stands. But the music of falling water is everywhere, and if you stand on the bridge, you can watch white foam spilling in luxurious cascades over ledges of stepped shale.

As I stand here on a warm October day, a few people come and go, stopping briefly to get out of their cars, aim their cameras, and exclaim at the beauty of the falls. "You'd have to drive a long way to see something this beautiful," says one, a man in a shiny sky-blue driving jacket, standing beside me and pointing his video camera at the falls. I nod, smile, and wait politely for him to finish. I'm all thumbs with cameras and have long since given up trying to photograph such places. Instead, I try to let the place come into me, impress itself on the negative of my memory.

What I see at first is not the present moment but layers of the past, as if this moment were just another dab of paint on an old canvas. Once, there were a dozen or more grinding mills in this area, where water spills from a dam less than a mile away. A hundred years ago, this place was busy grinding the corn of local farms and sawing the lumber of nearby forests. All that remains is a four-story building below the falls, owned by "someone from the city," I'm told, meaning someone from Rochester. The old mill has been turned into a residence. It is empty now, silently contemplating the falls.

But the genius loci of this place is still one of happy industry. To my left, a brick power plant built in 1922 houses a water wheel generating five hundred to a thousand kilowatts of electricity every day. It's one of the oldest of seven such hydroelectric plants supplying power to the area; there are five in Rochester alone. The falling water turning the horizontal blades of the wheel inside the building is still a free source of power. And it destroys no trees, poisons no sky, no earth, no wind.

Here in what was once the millrace is room and enough soil for wild roses, purple asters, milkweed, goldenrod, and Scotch thistle to grow. Stately rushes raise seed heads to sway gracefully in the breeze made by the falls. A patch of willows holds a little island. Wild mint grows in the shallows—I smell it when my boot crushes a stem of it as I pass. Hemlock grow up the hill on either side of the stream. An impressive array of beech, oak, maple, and sycamore fill the hillside; they are what make this such a popular spot in autumn. Their leaves weave a tapestry in rich threads of scarlet, persimmon, apricot, and bronze.

I take my lunch by the stream, sitting on one of the hundreds of rocks in the mill run, listening, imagining the sound of horse-drawn wagons pulling up to the mill, filled with corn ready to be ground. The water falling over the shallow cliffs reminds me of the lace on a bridal veil. In some places, water spills over tiny ledges and makes dainty, miniature falls, complete with foam and eddies on a Lilliputian scale. Looking up-stream, I can see the wall of water plunging over the dam. At the base of the drop point closest to the bridge is an almost perfectly round hole in the shale several feet deep, like a well, whether man-made or natural I cannot tell. It gives the place a distinctly baptismal air.

Climbing the steep path to the highest drop point of the falls, I watch yellow oak leaves bright as coins stick to the rocks under the water. The sycamores on the hilltops rain gold in the breeze. I sit down again and listen for a long time, alone. The music of falling water is constant and soothing. This is the song we live by, the rush of water and the soft splash of foam. This is the music of life.

Ice Age

Water never forgets it was once ice.
JAMES TREFIL,
Meditations at 10,000 Feet

Police radios buzzed and red flares sputtered around me in the darkness of a December night in 1985. My wrecked Subaru lay some ten yards away, like a great wounded turtle turned helplessly on its back.

I had been heading up a hill on Pennsylvania Route 219 South when I felt the right front tire of my car slide on an invisible patch of black ice. The steering wheel twirled in my hands as the car skidded off the road and up an embankment. Then the car turned over. I knew that two tons of steel were about to collide upside down with the pavement. I knew this was the sort of accident that often results in a broken neck.

I was flying into blackness, wondering if I had already died.

It was then I had the strange sensation that there was someone in the empty seat next to me who turned to speak in words that seemed to form inside my head. *Not yet*, said the mysterious voice. *It's not your time.*

The car landed with a jolt, skidded a few yards, and stopped. I was upside down. The roof of the car was on the ground. I felt cold air rushing in from the spaces where the windshields had been.

I heard tires squealing behind me, footsteps running, and a

woman's voice crying out in the darkness. "Are you all right?"

It was some moments before I could speak. "I think so," I said finally.

"Thank God—can you get out?"

I could feel my legs pressed up against the steering wheel and realized I was alive. I moved my arms and found I was covered with soft flakes of the shattered glass that had once been the windshields of the car. The glassy white flakes pooled in my lap and on the stiff gray wool of my overcoat. I turned and pushed an elbow against the car door. It was jammed shut.

"I can't open the door."

"I think you can get out back here." I turned my head and saw that the woman speaking to me was kneeling behind the car, where the back windshield had once been. She held out her hand through the opening. "Go on," she said. "Take my hand." I wondered about the possibility of gasoline leaking and the car exploding, and I wondered at the courage of the woman kneeling on the cold pavement a few feet away. She waited while I gathered my wits enough to move. "I'm here," she said. "Come on, you can do it. Try to grab hold of my hand."

As more cars arrived and the smoky red flares appeared around us, I finally managed to twist myself around to crawl on my hands and knees along the roof of the car and out the back window. I held on to the hands of the woman, who helped me to stand and walk away from the wreck. Free of the car, I looked back and saw that it lay just off the road on a narrow strip of berm, opposite from the side that I had been traveling. The road turned sharply just ahead, and if the car had been anywhere else, there could have been another accident when an unsuspecting motorist came around the turn.

The woman whose name I never learned walked me to the

door of an ambulance that had just pulled up behind us. In the miniature hospital on board the paramedics checked me over, and when they determined I was not injured, one of them gave me a cigarette to calm my nerves. I hadn't smoked for years, but that night it was a blessing. They drove me off to the hospital for X-rays before I could thank the woman who had shown so much kindness. I think they were unable to believe that I had survived such an accident without a scratch. But the X-rays showed nothing.

The next day I went to the wrecker's garage to collect my belongings from the car, or what was left of it. The twisted shell of the Subaru was turned right side up again, and I could clearly see that the roof on the passenger's side was pushed in almost a foot toward the seat—more than enough to strike the head of a passenger, had there been one. When the car flipped, it came down on that empty passenger's side, rather than on the driver's side, where the impact surely would have broken my neck.

"You must have the angels on your side," I heard someone say. I turned to look at a stocky man in greasy overalls who smiled and winked at me. His name was Clayt, and he had the wrecking business cornered in town—his garage was full of other twisted automobiles. Mine, he said, was a certified total wreck. It would be sold for scrap by the insurance company. He gave me a cardboard box holding what was left: the car stereo and a few tapes, the license plate, and a pair of shoes I'd had in the car.

I thanked Clayt and shook his hand. I didn't tell him, yes, I believe in angels, now. Angels of snow, angels of ice. Angels with eyes in the darkness and the power to lift and turn two tons of steel as it flies through the air, to set it down just off the road, out of danger. Angels with the voices of women.

The next two days I spent at home, alone. I didn't have a car anymore, so I couldn't run the long list of errands I always made for myself. I took some time off from teaching and canceled the holiday parties I had been planning. While I was waiting for the insurance adjustor's claims to be processed, I passed the time reading a book I'd received for Christmas the year before and had never opened because I had been too busy. It was the *Collected Poems of Emily Dickinson*. One of the poems was titled "Called Back."

Just lost when I was saved!
Just felt the world go by!
Just girt me for the onset of eternity,
When breath blew back,
And on the other side
I heard recede the disappointed tide!

Since then I calculate my age starting anew with the night of the accident. Today I am ten years old.

This morning, on the anniversary of the accident, there is a veneer of ice glittering on the boards of the deck outside my bedroom. I open the door and reach out my hand, brushing my palm across the ice, and it melts wet and oily on my warm skin. Ice gilds the evergreens in our yard, banding the holly with frost, tipping the needles of the dwarf pines white, painting the creeping myrtle stiff and glossy.

On my way to work, I drive by a pasture where two horses stand as if frozen, a bay mare and a shaggy chestnut pony. Their shoulders are cloaked with crystalline mantles of frost. They are so lovely in the still, cold morning that I turn around and pull my car off the road to look at them. The pony nods its head to me, ambling toward the fence. From the nostrils of both horses comes their breath, white and steamy, little clouds.

In the sky above us are altocumulus clouds, scalloped waves I know mean snow will be falling sometime within the next twenty-four hours. The clouds are high up, twenty thousand feet up in the sky. The water they release will be frozen ice crystals brushing together to make snowflakes as they fall toward the earth. Sometimes the snow is round pellets, made very high up in the cold clouds. Sometimes it is wet, flat, sticky flakes, from warmer clouds nearer the earth. Sometimes it is thick and feathery, so dense it can blind you. This is the snow I find most beautiful. It is the kind I always picture now when I hear Liszt's "Concert Etude" for the piano. I once listened to this music on my car stereo as I drove at dusk through snow that fell like lacy arpeggios in time with the music's descending octaves.

The snow falls, piling up around our house, and then it melts. Then it freezes again to make ice. Walking down our street in January, I listen to the groan and drip of the ice, an accompaniment to the screech of schoolchildren's laughter as they skid along on the slick sidewalks, the squeal of tires and the slamming of front doors as the town gets to work. Snow and ice pile up on rooftops, and the warmth escaping from the poorly insulated hundred-year-old houses makes the ice drip in spectacular stalactites festooning rococo Victorian rafters. Later, as I walk home, it is the sound of picks and shovels I hear as workmen hack at the ice on sidewalks, cracking it into shards and sweeping it into piles of what look like broken glass.

On days like this there is a crystalline quality to the air, tiny frozen crystals of snow falling from clouds that must be very high. I picture the descent of these crystals as they slip through layers of shivering space in the swirling cold country of wind currents and hawks, landing finally on our pond, miles out of town. In winter it is a silent disk of silver, keeping its frozen secrets.

There must be a moment, on the darkest night of the year, when the pond's surface becomes solid, when the tetrahedrons of water molecules are sufficiently cooled to become ice. But no one sees it. No one has skated on it for years now. The young people who once skated across the pond are gone, and we have become townspeople.

But we all still live in an age of ice. Water capping the North Pole is locked in ice. The continent of Antarctica, the island of Greenland, and large portions of Canada and Siberia are solid with permafrost. Only ten thousand years ago, a vast sheet of ice covered Canada and crept down over what is now Wisconsin, Minnesota, Michigan, Ohio, New York, and Massachusetts. Glaciers a mile thick carved the land into oval-shaped drumlins, ridge-shaped moraines, and conical hills called kames. Ice sculpting depressions out of rock made the Great Lakes. The power of such ice is almost unimaginable. Solid, frozen, moving, a glacier can shear off the top of a mountain, throwing boulders as if they were pebbles, leaving piles of gravel behind. Its fingers scrape lakes from valleys and scour kettle-shaped bowls from hills. The great glaciers are receding, but they have not melted, not entirely. They still cover one-tenth of the earth's surface.

On the South Pole, ice twenty thousand years old is a time capsule of information. We can remove cores of the ice to read the Ice Age record. The ice formed during the decade of the 1980s reveals more of the polluting "greenhouse" gases of carbon dioxide, methane, and nitrous oxide in the ice than at any other time. In 1988, one of the warmest years on record, NASA's James Hansen testified to the U.S. Senate that the average temperature of the earth had increased one degree Fahrenheit over the past century and that the six warmest of those years had occurred in that very decade: they were 1980, 1981, 1983, 1986, 1987, and 1988. One more degree's increase in the earth's temperature—the projected outcome if the greenhouse gases trapping radiation in the atmosphere were allowed to continue growing—could melt the ice and cause the seas to rise. The coastlines of our continents would shrink, and the forests would die.

But the summer of 1991 was one of the coolest on record. And geological records indicate that the earth was once even warmer. Long before the industrial revolution, the levels of oceans and lakes were much higher. Greenland was truly green, and salty seas covered Death Valley and the Bonne-ville Flats.

No one is certain what causes these drastic changes in climate. Perhaps solar flares—sunspots—cause more radiation to reach the earth at some times. Perhaps the earth's shifts in the wobbling tilt of its axis, along with changes in its orbit around the sun, cause corresponding increases and decreases in the amounts of sunlight the planet receives. Volcanoes and even meteorites affect the atmosphere, pushing the jet streams around, dumping rain in some places while others suffer drought.

Where I live, the winter of 1993 was one of the coldest on record. It was followed by one of the warmest. The winter of 1995–96 broke the records for snowfall.

The ice grows, moves, melts, and recedes through the ages, maestro of its own mysterious music.

Those who love trees hate the ice. Ice storms can devastate a forest, gripping the branches of its trees in a deep freeze. A year ago we lost the oldest apple tree in our yard. It gave in to the last of winter's storms, submitting in the night to the weight of the ice. We found it bowed on the lawn the next morning like a supplicant, head to the ground, arms spread sideways, silent. What did it pray for? What transformation?

The ice storm of March 1991 left some twenty thousand customers of the New York State Electric and Gas Company without power, many for several weeks. It was the worst ice storm since 1936, when the headline on the *Alfred Sun* read "Terrific Ice Storm Visits Alfred and Vicinity." The 1991 ice storm issue carried the banner headline "Operation Ice Storm Devastates Alfred-Almond Area," a pun on the military campaign against Iraq that same year.

The storm began on the evening of March 4, coating trees, power lines, and utility poles with ice so heavy that by midnight everything began to break. In the middle of the night, Bill and I heard tree branches scrape on the roof. We were living in Alfred at the time, renting an old farmhouse with freestanding gas heaters that kept us warm through the night. We didn't know the power was out until we rose early that morning and tried to turn on lights.

It was then the real bombardment began. Every few minutes, we heard a crack and a pop like the report of a rifle. It was the sound of tree limbs breaking, split with the weight of the ice. Emergency crews roamed the village to clear the roads of fallen limbs. Like old-fashioned town criers, they called out from the passing fire trucks with megaphones, telling us to conserve water because the village's electric water pumps were without power. People who had electric thermostats on their gas furnaces were in the same predicament and without heat.

We went out to clear the fallen tree limbs from our driveway. Curious to see how the trees in our backyard had fared, Bill strolled around the house. I turned to see him walking toward the maple tree behind our kitchen door, and I heard the tree groan. I screamed, and Bill hit the ground, diving to escape the falling treetop.

We decided to let the road crews roaming the streets take over the job of clearing fallen trees. The job took weeks, and there are places that still show the scars of trees bent and fallen with the ice.

Yet each time I hear the wind in the night and the scrape of ice falling on the roof, I am bound to go out the next morning. Each time, there is a moment of grace when the forest in winter is lifted up in a frozen transfiguration, a death I cannot deny is beautiful.

It is after midnight on the first of February this year that I hear wind sweeping dampness into ice after a long day of rain. I have a bad cold, and all night I toss with fever, dreaming of the hemlocks in our yard growing long, sweeping shawls of ice. As early as it is safe, I dress and go out to my car. I head up Jericho Hill, the highest point in the county. The car stereo whispers with the restless sigh of synthesizer music.

I reach the crest of the hill and turn off the stereo, pull the car off the road, and come to a stop near a lane that leads away from the road and into the woods. I look up at a forest of black branches beaded with crystal, shimmering in the opalescent light of morning. The landscape spread out before me is made of cool, pale shades like the transparent brush strokes of a watercolor painted in ice, stiff yellow grasses bent by the wind on the frozen white page of the snow. Under a stand of pines, inside a fence leaning into the wind, each stalk, seed, nettle, and vine in the abandoned pasture has a silver coat of ice. A row of brittle Queen Anne's lace glides along in front of the fence, ice dancers in a regal saraband of ice, heads raised stiffly to the sky. A little further along the crest of the hill, the larger trees are blooming with ice, the white pine thrusting out needles blue with ice, the hemlocks wearing glassy glissandos of ice, the spruce draped with long arpeggios of ice, a whole forest of ice sparkling silver against the sky that shimmers with the pink and blue light of morning.

The black branch of the sycamore at the top of the hill is calligraphic against the pale sky. I hear something call, like wind whistling through a pipe of crystal. I have heard it said that cold intensifies the upper registers of sound, muting the lower tones just as snow muffles the ring of a boot on the walk. In winter the higher tones reach us more clearly, insistently.

I know of at least one other who heard the song of the ice.

He loved the ice. Each winter, he measured the ice on Walden Pond and listened to its "whoop" and "groan" as it shifted, expanded, and broke. Once, the ice that formed on ponds like Thoreau's Walden was cut and loaded onto horse-drawn barges, hauled off the "azure tinted marble" of the pond to an ice house shielded with straw, and saved there until summer to cool a gentleman's drink. Thoreau lamented the ice cutters taking the pond's only coat. But Walden had its revenge when one of them fell into the water or a plow broke on the hard surface of the pond.

On a good day, they took a thousand tons of ice, and it would be sold, he imagined, to "the sweltering inhabitants of

Charleston and New Orleans," who paid a luxury price for their cool mint juleps, their sorbets of jasmine and rose, their iced creams of tangerine, peach, and melon. Flowers and dolls were frozen in blocks of the ice and used as centerpieces to cool the tropical air of the South. The ice was sent as far away as Britain, where a block of it in a London shop window attracted crowds.

Thoreau measured the length and angle of ice on the weeds and grasses of the fields around Walden Pond, marking the "divinity" within them, the "prisms" of blue, violet, and red made in the ice when the sun illuminated it. He walked ice-covered fields where he saw "each twig and needle thickly encrusted with ice, one vast gelid mass, which our feet crunch, as if we were walking through the cellar of some confectioner to the gods." He saw the ice-covered trees and "the transparent ice, like a thick varnish," shining on their bark. "All objects are to the eye polished silver," he wrote in his journal. "It is a perfect land of faery."

He found beauty in every aspect of winter, in its violet mists and silver skies. Its snowflakes, he thought, should be called "snow stars" or "wheels of the storm chariots." He meditated on the snowflakes as on any other creation of nature. "There they lie," he wrote, "like the wreck of chariot wheels after a battle in the skies. . . . And they all sing, melting as they sing, of the mysteries of the number six; six, six, six . . . pronouncing order."

I wander off the road along the lane, pondering this promise of order—*six, six, six*. Each ice crystal is hexagonal, six hydrogen atoms forming the bond that links the oxygen in a madrigal of molecules we call ice.

Beside the lane lined with red maple, under the trees, a

stream trickles through narrow borders of ice frozen in curling rivulet patterns against either bank. The ice is etched with a design of scrolled waves like those I have seen in Chinese ink drawings of water. It is a design meant to indicate movement, but it is frozen now in its swirling rite, its promise that nothing ever dies but only takes another form, dances another dance.

This too is life. For a moment, the atoms of ice and water dance together, the ice along the bank where no turbulence stirs the temperature of the water, the water keeping its liquid state in the stream where constant movement prevents it from freezing. The ground pine at my feet is miraculously green, and when I pull down a branch of the maple over my head, I can see the new red bud encased in its cocoon of ice.

Baptism by Fire

An inward baptism of pure fire
Tis all my longing soul's desire.
PENNSYLVANIA DUTCH BAPTISMAL CERTIFICATE 1891

On December 1, sleet coats the house with gray ice, and there are more hours of darkness than of light. All day, I keep logs of locust, maple, and oak from our woodpile burning in the fireplace. As I sit by the fire, working on the notes for a lecture, the burning oak sends a wall of heat to my face, and I look up to see bright fingers of flame, blue at the base, twisting into sinuous golden tips. The logs gasp and spit as pockets of air in the gnarled wood explode with the heat. When they are very hot, the logs glow from within, turning white, and suddenly all that's left are the coals glowing red. I put on more logs, stir the embers, and watch the fire renewing itself in a leaping and swaying dance of transformation. I think of the dance of Shiva, who holds fire in his left hand, beating the drum of creation with his right. Surrounded by a ring of fire, he is both creator and destroyer.

I wonder how many million times human eyes have gazed into a fire and seen a vision of heaven or hell, a phantom of delight or despair, the formlessness of chaos or the revelation of the divine. Like the gods of the Orient, where the sacred has many faces, many forms, fire can be angel or devil, creator or destroyer, saint or sinner, friend or enemy, servant or master. We can reduce it to a technical description: "Fire is the rapid chemical combination of oxygen with the carbon and other elements of organic substances so that heat, flame, and light are produced." But we can never describe its power. There is no other element so ambiguous or so potent in its ability to destroy and to transform, to warm, to work, to frighten, to soothe.

Bill and I spent some time looking for a house with a fireplace, for many people no longer think of fire as essential. A fireplace and a chimney add expense to a construction plan, taking up space. It's true we don't actually need fire to heat our home. A gas furnace sends hot water around the baseboard registers in the room. The chimney wastes heat, sending a cold draft into the room more often than not. But in our dark, cold corner of the Northeast, the bright flame of a fire provides psychological warmth. More than its heat, we need the sense of security it brings, the ancient memory of a torch carried against the darkness, the great gift stolen from the gods.

The designer of the house we finally purchased knew fire's aesthetic value. He placed the brick-lined hearth at the focal point of the living room, facing it with creamy marble and gleaming brass to reflect the bright flames of a fire in the room. On the short days of the winter season, the dancing flames of a fire in the hearth lift my mood. We keep a good supply of firewood, cut mainly from our own woodlots. Wood from the locust tree we cut down last year makes a fragrant, warm fire. Ash fires are pungent, and cherry wood burns sweet. Oak logs make a strong, hot, long-lasting fire.

When snow surrounds the house at the holidays, fire makes

a colorful scene indoors. Expecting guests, we build a fire to greet them. Our friends are drawn to the fire's bright welcome, sipping coffee and brandy, speaking with us in quiet, relaxed voices, their faces shining in the firelight. Sitting around the fire, they feel immediately at home.

There have been hearths as long as there have been people walking upright, and anthropologists suspect that many of the oldest hearths—those over two hundred thousand years old—were used for ritual. Fire is an archetypal symbol of the divine. The Upanishads say, "As Sparks innumerable fly upward from a blazing fire, so from the depths of the Imperishable arise all things." In the Bhagava Gita, Krishna says, "I am the fire residing in the bodies of all things which have life." Agni, the Hindu fire god, is son of Heaven and Earth. He is so voracious that he devours both mother and father on being born. Agni's flame, held in the left hand of Shiva, is the transforming element: "As the sun purifies all Nature with his light and heat, so Agni shall purify everything which enters his flame."

The heat of a fire symbolizes the passion of spiritual faith. God spoke to Abraham from a burning bush. A flame burns at the center of the sacred heart of Christ. On the day of the Pentecost, the fervor of the Holy Spirit descended on his disciples in the form of "cloven tongues like as of fire." George Fox, founder of the Quakers, described his inspiration to reform the church as a holy fire: "There did a pure fire appear in me . . . his holy refining fire" A Hindu mantra says, "O Fire, yours is the power to penetrate the innermost recesses of the human heart and discover its truth." And Saint Paul says, "Every man's work shall be made manifest: for the day shall declare it, because it shall be revealed by fire; and the fire shall try every man's work of what sort it is."

Fire has long been used as punishment for falsehoods and disloyalty. Nebuchadnezzar, king of Babylon, threw Shadrach, Meshach, and Abednego into the fiery furnace when they would not worship his gods. But the God of Israel saved them, and they walked through the fire unharmed, for they had shown the ultimate loyalty. In medieval societies, the "trial by fire" was used to judge the testimony of criminals who pleaded innocence. The accused would be forced to walk through fire, put a hand in the fire, or grasp an ingot red hot with fire. It was thought that those who were truly innocent could not be harmed by the fire. Fire was the ultimate punishment for heretics.

Dante condemned "false counselors" or traitors to be swathed in fire. In his inferno, each of the condemned souls is itself a flame, and the poet sees thousands of these flames moving through the valley of the damned. There are so many that he describes them as fireflies gleaming in the fields of a vineyard:

> *Quante il villan ch'al poggio si reposa . . .*
> *veded lucciole gui per la vallea,*
> *forse cola dov'e vendemmia ed ara:*
> *di tante fiamme tuta risplendea*
> *l'ottava bolgia . . .*

Loki, the great trickster god of the Norse, was a fire demon, born in a forest fire. Loki charmed both men and women with his lies. He often sat in the great halls of the gods and was a sworn blood brother to Odin. Jealous, vengeful, destructive, Loki was fond of remorselessly pitting one divine colleague against the other with his treachery.

In the Old Testament, fire is the wrath of God. Eden is guarded by angels holding flaming swords, fiery serpents attack the Israelites when they denounce Jehovah. Moses tells his people, "The Lord thy God is a consuming fire" and "Out of heaven he made thee to hear his voice, that he might instruct thee: and upon earth he shewed thee his great fire; and thou heardest his words out of the midst of fire."

It is not surprising that the prophet of Revelation describes the end of the world in the fearsome terms of a great firestorm, when "whosoever was not found written in the book of life was cast into the lake of fire." Fire historian Stephen Pyne points out that people of biblical times probably witnessed fires that gave them the inspiration for their metaphors. "The darkness and the roar," he writes, "the streams of aerial fire and the scenes of devastation depicted by biblical prophets all are properties of mass fires, and the literary descriptions probably derive from experiences with large fires in the brush fields of the Near East."

"Earth is a fire planet, and Homo sapiens, a fire creature," says Pyne, author of *Fire and Civilization.* Just as I type these words, the scream of fire engines sears the air. It is a sound I hear often here in winter. I go outside to look for signs of smoke, but I don't see any. Only later, I read in the news that Maynard Ayers, eighty-six, founder of our local drug and alcohol treatment center, suffered third-degree burns when he tried to put out a kitchen fire at his home on the other side of town.

One of my earliest memories is of a fire in the house next

door to the one where I was born. I must have been two or three years old. Our house was separated from the one next door only by a narrow alley. I was carried outside late at night, and I remember being held up high in my mother's arms. I was in my nightclothes, and I felt the cold air and breathed the acrid smell of smoke. I saw the firemen bringing a woman out of the house next door on a stretcher. I heard my mother curse and understood her saying that the woman had probably fallen asleep drunk, smoking a cigarette in bed. I was surprised at my mother's tone; I had not heard such bitterness towards another person before from her lips. There must have been some danger that our old house would also catch fire. I remember a brightness, and many people gathered on the sidewalk, more than I had ever seen there. I must have fallen asleep again in my mother's arms, for I don't remember going back inside.

A fire on your own property leaves an even longer shadow against memory. I open a box of books long stored in the garage, and the smell of an old fire greets me. The books had been packed in a sturdy cardboard box of the kind publishers use for shipping them. I acquired some of these boxes when I moved from Pennsylvania in the summer of 1989, and I used them to store my books in a building Bill uses as his art studio. The night of August 17, 1989, was unseasonably cold, and there was an eclipse of the moon. I remember shivering in a wool sweater as we stood on a hilltop outside of town, watching the moon disappear.

The heater at the studio must have come on in the night, and the old wiring shorted and sparked. The fire smoldered through the night, finally breaking out into flames and smoke around 6:00 A.M. By pure chance, I had put my boxes of books in a corner, far from the place where the fire broke out over the heater, blackening everything nearby. The fire must have licked at the box, however, for the edges of each paperback book are faintly brown, and the waxed covers have melted just enough to stick together. Virginia Woolf is stuck to William Gass, and Lawrence Durrell melts against Carson McCullers. I pry the covers gently apart and put them in alphabetical order on the bookshelf. Woolf goes at the far end of the row of novels, Gass and McCullers in the middle, and Durrel towards the beginning, next to Kate Chopin, who escaped the fire. Her book was in my office at the university, while the others were in storage.

A writer arriving early at the newspaper office next to Bill's studio saw the fire and called in the alarm. A clay sculpture of Janus on a pedestal by the door was one of the first casualties, smashed to pieces as firemen broke down the door. Janus is supposed to guard doorways. With two faces, one looking to the past, and one to the future, Janus is usually portrayed as male. This Janus, a female form, had the sense to give way and allow the firemen to rush in and remove an acetylene torch that could have blown the roof off had the fire reached it.

Forms in wax long rejected as sculptures—Bill uses the lost wax process for his bronze sculptures—were melted blobs on the shelves. Luckily, his most recent work, a life-size bronze of King Alfred, was not yet worked in wax. The small plastilene model had just begun to feel the heat of the fire on the second floor when the firemen arrived. Holding his miniature sword aloft bravely, he lost only a hand and part of a nose, easily restored with plastilene surgery.

We are not always so fortunate. Fire is responsible for the

deaths of some six thousand civilians and as many as a hundred firefighters each year in the United States. It destroys billions of dollars worth of property. Statistics for 1992 show that in New York State, there were 164,940 fires, 322 deaths, and well over a billion dollars of property damage. There were 251 fires in our county, with an estimated dollar loss of over three million dollars. Statewide, the number of fires and the number of fire-related deaths have dropped steadily over the past decade, the result of smoke detectors and improved fire codes, mandated by the Uniform Fire Prevention and Building Code.

But the number of civilians injured while trying to put out fires has increased. Three days after being taken to the hospital, Maynard Ayers died from his burns. Too many people like him try to control a small fire themselves first before calling the fire department.

Cooking, heating, and "incendiary/suspicious" are the leading causes of the fires that cause injuries. So many fires are of "suspicious origin," as the fire officials put it, that it is difficult to know how many are accidental and how many the result of arson. But some experts estimate that as many as three-quarters of all fires in the United States can be attributed to arson, the highest rate in the world. According to FBI statistics, young people—mostly males—are responsible for a full 50 percent of all arson, and half of those arsonists are under the age of fifteen. Unsupervised children are often responsible for setting fires by accident when they play with matches, fascinated with fire's beautiful, bright face, not comprehending the danger. Lack of experience with fire may also make fire intriguing for older children acting out feelings of powerlessness.

Statistically, our insurance agent tells us, we should not have to worry about another fire on our own property. Most people don't suffer more than one in a lifetime. A thorough insurance policy pays for renovations, and the building is actually in better shape once the repairs are finished. But we listen more attentively to fire alarms now.

Leaving the English department office at Alfred University a little before noon on a Friday in November, I hear the village emergency alarm sounding. It's a little early, but at first I think it is only the daily practice alarm that always rings at noon. The alarm keeps blaring, however, and as I walk through the parking lot, I see a plume of smoke rising from behind the white spire of the Seventh Day Baptist Church. I walk toward the scene, but it has already been blocked off by the volunteer firemen. I get close enough to see flames shooting up from a tree growing close to the burning building. The tree is burning too, a bright red candle on the lawn. Still several blocks away, I can smell the smoke. Black flakes of ash fall on my red jacket, drifting through the cold air like sooty snow.

It takes six hours to put out the fire because the tin roof and aluminum siding on the house trap heat inside. Four students have escaped with their lives, but all their possessions are lost—clothes, books, wallets, even their shoes. One ran out in his pajamas, the firefighters tell me, shaken awake in time by a housemate. The building code for rentals constructed before 1950 had not required either smoke alarms or fire extinguishers, so the landlord hadn't bothered to provide them.

That night, I stand with a group of lingering bystanders watching inspectors begin their search for a cause. They tiptoe through the building, shining flashlights into the black-ened jumble that was once a home. The four students are given rooms in a dorm, the church donates clothing, and the American Red Cross gives them gift certificates to purchase a few essential items from nearby stores. Later, the fire depart-ment decides the fire was caused by a gas leak.

In a few weeks, the site has been cleared of debris all the way down to the foundation, and a new rental unit is soon erected in its place. This one is equipped with smoke detectors.

Although accidents or arson are responsible for many fires, nature also causes fires in what many scientists maintain is a cycle of cleansing and rebirth. According to entomologists Robert Haack and William Mattson, a rain-starved tree ac-tually signals its distress with ultrasonic sounds caused by water columns breaking in the sapwood. The tree's tempera-ture rises, its leaves changing color in the infrared frequencies perceptible to insects ready to move in and find homes. Once damaged sufficiently by drought and opportunistic insects, a dying forest can become a healthy, growing entity once again only in a baptism by fire.

In 1988, after a summer-long drought, lightning started wildfires in Yellowstone National Park. The fires eventually destroyed five million acres. In a fire this size, the tallest trees tumble and burn as easily as toothpicks, smoke obscures the sun, and fireballs drop unexpectedly from the sky like rock-ets. The hellish maelstrom can generate winds of up to 80 miles an hour.

But once it was over, the ash of the great fire fertilized the soil, and new, green growth appeared within weeks. Certain trees, such as the sequoia and some pines, need the heat of a fire to release seeds from their cones. And some birds will build their nests only on the lower, fire-cleared branches of pine trees.

Some scientists believe that fire prevention has actually thwarted nature's ecological cycle of smaller fires that clear the forests of the fallen tree limbs, dead wood, twigs, and drought-dried brush on a regular basis. The buildup of tinder results in more widespread fires like those at Yellowstone in 1988 and those in the far West in 1994, which killed twenty-five people, including several firefighters. Smaller fires allowed to burn now and then could have prevented these disasters—they are nature's way of fighting fire with fire. Fire even promotes biodiversity by eliminating non-native opportunistic species that choke out space and sun and allowing room for natives to regenerate. Places where fire is regularly suppressed, says Stephen Pyne, are "suffering from fire famine."

Our primal need for fire is reflected in our myths. Prometheus, son of a Titan and a water nymph, created man by forming clay from earth and water and then firing it. His name means "forethought." To aid men in their advance, he stole the fire so jealously guarded at Olympus by Zeus and carried it to earth in the hollow reed of a fennel stalk. Enraged, Zeus meted on him a horrible punishment, one equal to the importance of fire. He lashed Prometheus to a rock on the top of a mountain, with a vulture feeding on his liver. Prometheus was finally rescued by the great hero Hercules.

Ancient people had no easy way to strike a fire whenever they needed one. So a sacred fire was kept burning somewhere at all times. The responsibility for the fire was given to a high official, and in early Rome, a cult emerged made up of young girls who tended the sacred fires. They were dedicated to worshiping Vesta, the beautiful "bright-faced" goddess of the hearth. During the time of the Roman republic, the cult became an institution. Six Vestal Virgins, women chosen in youth from patrician families, tended the shrine of Vesta where the sacred fire burned. Their purity was important. If found guilty of relinquishing their virginity, they could be shut up to die in an underground cell. So high was their status in Roman society that even the officers of the legions saluted them.

Vesta, or Hestia, as she has come to be known, is actually a gentle, domestic goddess, usually represented not by a virgin but by the figure of a loving mother tending the hearth. Her name comes from a Sanskrit root, *vas*, meaning "shining." The fire of Hestia nourishes and protects her children.

The hearth at our house in town is mainly decorative, but at our cabin outside of town, we still rely on fire for light and warmth. On a bright, cold December day, when wind stirs the boughs of the Norway spruce and a fresh coat of snow paints the brown field of the pasture white, we have come to fix the clogged drainpipe in the pond before the winter's frosts destroy it. But before we begin to work, we start a fire in the cabin's old pot-bellied stove. We lay in dry sticks gathered from the woods, crumpled newspaper, and small logs of locust wood cut from one of the trees outside our house in town. I know the fire is alive at the moment I hear the chimney pipe sing as it expands with the heat rising from the stove.

Back outside, we work for over an hour in the mud on the edge of the pond, siphoning cold water in the runoff to the creek to drop the level of the pond back to the top of the clogged drainpipe. Then we clear the muck blocking the pipe, a brisk wind blowing on us the whole time. The system of pipes Bill has devised for the runoff works perfectly, and the water level returns to normal. We gather up our tools and hurry back to the cabin.

The sweet smell of the locust wood burning in the stove greets us as we pull off our muddy boots. We are still shivering. Behind the nine rectangles of isinglass set in the door to the stove, the fire roars orange and blue. We stretch out our hands to it, and we are warm.

Home

Stand still.
The trees ahead and bushes beside you
Are not lost.
Wherever you are is called Here.
DAVID WAGONER, "Lost"

Where is home? One definition is "a place of origin," the place where you were born. I was born in the city of Pittsburgh, on the Allegheny plateau, at the place where the Allegheny, Monongahela, and Ohio Rivers meet, in Allegheny County. Forty-five years later I'm still perched on the same plateau, now at the very northeastern tip of it. Here, the county I live in is named Allegany but spelled differently. I've planted myself in almost the same climate, the same topography, the same kind of wet river valley as the one where I was born.

Last spring, I planted a little of the soil from the place where I was born in my new Allegany County home. I had been visiting my parents in Pittsburgh the week before, admiring the hydrangeas around their home. "Take some," my mother told me. "They're too big now, anyway. It's time they were divided." These bushes were already once removed from her own father's plants, like much of what grows in her yard. When her house was built, she brought cuttings and shoots from her father, Salvatore's, extensive gardens, roots wrapped in sheets of newspapers, damp and warm with the soil of her father's home. She tells me the story of how he acquired the hydrangeas—he had planted them in one of his client's yards, but for some reason they never bloomed. "Take them out!" the client impatiently demanded. So they went to Salvatore's home, where they gladly bloomed. Perhaps they were more at home there.

As I divided one of the bushes with a spade, cutting off a small chunk of the plant, I thought of Salvatore, and when I took the plant out of the car six hours later and two hundred miles to the north, I imagined him watching me, dressed in his work clothes as I used to see him, a half-smile of pleasure playing on his face. I dug a new hole beside our backyard fence, filled the hole with compost, and eased the plant into its new home, the earth from my mother's yard still clinging to its roots. I watered the plant in, and piled more dirt and more nitrogen-rich, crumbly black compost around it. Almost immediately, it began to thrive, producing lush, dark green leaves. This summer it produced gorgeous purple and blue flowers. It seems to be right at home.

Our house is sided in weathered cedar, making it seem to disappear into the trees around it, camouflaged like the bird nests I have found in the yard. They are abandoned homes, pieces of practical architecture but also miniature works of art which I can see only in fall when the trees are bare and the birds are gone. Some birds—woodpeckers, for instance—will reuse their nests, usually ones they have constructed deep within the hollow of a tree, where winter wind and snow cannot destroy them. Birds of prey such as hawks will rebuild their nests from year to year, enlarging them each time.

Some birds make no nests at all, laying their eggs right on the ground or, like the whippoorwill, on a soft bed of oak leaves.

My collection of abandoned bird nests is scattered about on the tops of tables and bureaus inside the house. I have several blue jay nests—"ragged affairs" they are called by the author of a 1902 text entitled *Bird Homes* that I find in the Wellsville library. The blue jay nests are made of loosely gathered twigs and roots, weeds, leaves, string, sometimes even shreds of plastic blown off someone's roof and wedged in a tree. In the branches of a Scotch pine that fell in our yard last winter, I found a house finch's nest, a shallow cup of twigs and leaves lined with grass and attached to a branch that was once high up in the pine. On ledges and over doorways I have found several robin's nests, deep cups molded of grass and mud. I love looking at these whorled bowls, each one as unique as its builder, each with its own artful shape and texture, small sculptures incorporating twigs and grass, milkweed fluff, roots, leaves. My favorite is the phoebe's pillowy nest, cushioned with the softest grass and decorated with fluffy bits of moss and lichen.

As I sit on our deck, looking out at the green swath of our yard, birds whose voices I have yet to identify are singing fiercely. I think of what Edward O. Wilson said in an interview with the Nature Conservancy last year: "Human beings gravitate toward what they consider to be the innately ideal human environment, namely a position atop a promontory overlooking a park-like savanna and a body of water . . . just the nearness or even the depiction of natural environments is psychologically restorative."

So I sit overlooking my little savanna. Our house is built

on the high side of the land that slopes down toward the river, giving us a hilltop perspective. Wind and water circulate around us, bringing what the Chinese call *ch'i*, the energy of life and luck. Masters of the art of feng shui still guide the placement of homes this way, tapping the flow of ch'i to bring the homeowners prosperity and good health. Inside, to keep the good ch'i circulating, we have house plants and bowls of water. One is a large orange glass bowl that is home to three goldfish, Chinese symbols of happiness. On the walls are scenes depicting the outdoors: a photograph of a grove of redwoods in California, an etching of tamarack trees, a large watercolor of blooming irises. From the french doors that face east, I can look out each morning and see what is here—birds and trees, rabbits and flowers and butterflies. Around us flow water and wind and sunlight, day by day, hour by hour, moment by moment.

Three Norway spruce shield the north side of our property, and in front of them a row of peonies marches, like those that I remember grew behind my grandfather's home. There is an ancient belief that peonies are magical emanations from the moon and if planted beside a home will protect it from tempests. This has so far been true of our peonies. They also yield abundant pink and white blooms every spring in spite of complete neglect. Peonies are so hardy, even in our brutal climate, that it is said they frequently outlive their owners.

As the summer solstice nears, I watch a honey bee already laden with pollen tirelessly working the peony blooms. The bee is collecting pollen in saddlebags made of the hairs on its hind legs. I can clearly see the golden pollen loaded into these bags, so heavy that the bee moves very slowly. Yet it tries one more flower before flying off, bearing its load of gold back to the hive. The pollen will be food for larvae and newly hatched young bees.

The grown bees eat honey made of the nectar collected from various flowers. Which flowers they have foraged will influence the color of their honey, for each nectar has a different tint and a different taste. Honey made mostly from buckwheat flowers is a dark reddish brown and has a strong flavor. I use it for making gingerbread. Orange blossom honey is golden, and clover honey is pale yellow, good for sweetening tea. Bees cluster on the yellow-green flowers of our basswood tree in June, and as I watch them I think of the basswood honey I'll buy at Kinfolk grocery store in Alfred come fall. With a rich golden hue and an exquisitely spicy flavor, it's as close to ambrosia as anything I've ever tasted. I don't know where the bees that make the honey I buy at Kinfolk get their nectar, but I like to think that some of it actually comes from the basswood tree outside my home.

The evening is warm, after a week of days so hot and humid that the weather service warns us to avoid exertion, stay indoors, and drink plenty of water. The air is laden with moisture that condenses overnight, and by dawn there is a mist soaking petal and stem, so that nothing wilts despite temperatures in the nineties. The morning mists soften everything, blurring the edges of flower and leaf. The humidity also intensifies smells, so that besides the sharp rose scent of the peonies I can also detect the smoky odor of hosta in the garden and the faint, sweet perfume of the white floribunda roses that grow behind our tomato patch.

At dusk I wait for the fireflies. It is dark enough now to see them, I think, if they are not a figment of my imagination, a ghostly dance of memory gone mad. I wonder if I was mistaken on the first two nights, for now there is only the occasional glint of last light on the leaf of a locust tree stirred by the breeze. It is the third night, and if I see them tonight, I have promised myself I will believe what I am seeing is real. I am prepared for disappointment—what business do fireflies have in pleasing me? At first I see only faint shadows moving, the bodies of insects traveling through the humid air. And then I see what I have been waiting for—a spark of light traveling high, twenty feet up along the line of pine trees bordering our yard, blinking in a straight line along the trees, as if drawing a curtain. I see another light curling across the yard, coming my way, and then another back by the vegetable garden, blinking off and on, then more and more flashes and sparks of light in the darkness until I can no longer count them.

There is nothing more magical on a summer evening than fireflies, nothing more like enchantment than their dance of tiny lights over the grass. I had hoped that they might bless this place with their presence, but until now I have never seen them here. Except in memory.

I remember fireflies flickering on the front lawn of my parents' home some thirty years ago. We called them lightning bugs, and my brother and I trapped them in glass pickle jars to watch them, blinking captives, before we let them go. Since then I have seen them once, flickering in the long grass of the meadow by the cabin outside of town, where we rarely mow. It was a magical night like this one at midsummer, when I thought I could feel the magnetic core of the earth sending waves of energy up through the soles of my feet as I walked through the long grass.

Now they are here, in my own yard. I peer at them, and

in the fading light I can occasionally make out the body of the insect. The firefly is a flying beetle, not a fly at all, with the phosphorescent lamp just under the tip of its abdomen flashing on and off as it flies above the grass. Both males and females have the gift, and they are signaling with it to the opposite sex, speaking the language of beetle love, saying sweet nothings to their mates.

The fireflies flashing above ground are the males, those waiting in the grasses below females. The males' eyes are adapted to searching the ground for their mates and sometimes have as many as twenty-five hundred hexagonal lenses in one eye, while the females may have only a few hundred. Each species of firefly has a distinctive flashing signal, some males flashing faster as they approach an answering female.

What would it be like, I wonder, to speak to your love in a language without words, to shine in the darkness of a summer night, beckoning with fingertips that glow in the dark?

Night falls, and stars come out to flicker above in the sky, as if in answer to the lights flickering on the lawn. Now I know I am home.